TEXTBOOK OF COMMUNITY PHARMACY

FOR PHARM. D

DR. CHALLA SRINIVAS REDDY , DR B .S. SHARVANA BHAVA, DR. SANTHI SREE VEMULAPALLI

Made with ♥ on the Notion Press Platform
www.notionpress.com

Contents

Textbook Of Community Pharmacy

For Pharm .D

Dr. Challa Srinivas Reddy, Principal & Professor
Vaagdevi College of Pharmacy,
Ramnagar, Hanamkonda, Warangal, Telangana, India
Dr. B.S. Sharvana Bhava, Professor & Head, Department of Clinical Pharmacy & Pharm.D.
Vaagdevi College of Pharmacy,
Ramnagar, Hanumakonda, Telangana, India
Dr. Santhi Sree Vemulapalli, Professor
Vijaya College of Pharmacy,
Hayatnagar, Munagnoor, India
Editor
Dr. Muralidhar Rao Akkaladevi, Principal
St. Mary's College of Pharmacy,
Secunderabad, Telangana
Published by Notion Press
Notion Press, Inc.
800, West El Camino Real #180,
California, USA 94040
Notion Press Media Pvt Ltd
#7, Red Cross Road,
Egmore, Chennai, Tamil Nadu 600008
Email ID: publish@notionpress.com
Phone Number: +91 44 46315631

Preface

The practice of community pharmacy has undergone significant transformations in recent years, reflecting the broader shifts within healthcare systems around the world. Pharmacists today are not merely dispensers of medications; they are vital healthcare providers who play a crucial role in patient care, health promotion, and disease prevention. This book, titled **"Textbook of Community Pharmacy: For Pharm.D,"** has been meticulously developed to serve as a comprehensive resource for Pharm.D students, educators, and practicing pharmacists who are committed to advancing their knowledge and skills in this dynamic field.

The creation of this textbook was motivated by the need for a resource that not only covers the technical aspects of community pharmacy but also delves deeply into the ethical, practical, and patient-centered responsibilities of pharmacists. This book provides a detailed exploration of key topics such as the principles of rational drug therapy, the intricacies of ethical decision-making, and the essential role of the pharmacist in community health. It is designed to bridge the gap between academic knowledge and real-world application, ensuring that readers are well-prepared to meet the challenges and opportunities of contemporary pharmacy practice.

Organized into thoughtfully structured chapters, this textbook covers the core components of community pharmacy practice. From foundational concepts and ethical guidelines to the management of minor ailments and the promotion of public health, each chapter is designed to provide a clear and comprehensive understanding of the subject matter. The content has been carefully curated to align with the Pharm.D curriculum, ensuring that it meets the educational needs of students while also serving as a valuable reference for practicing pharmacists.

A particular focus of this book is the application of ethical principles in everyday pharmacy practice. Pharmacists often face complex situations that require not only clinical expertise but also a strong ethical compass. This textbook provides practical guidance on navigating these challenges, emphasizing the importance of patient welfare, confidentiality, and professional integrity. Additionally, the book highlights the critical role of pharmacists in patient education, adherence monitoring, and the responsible use of medications, all of which are essential to achieving positive health outcomes.

This textbook is more than just an educational resource; it is a testament to the vital role that community pharmacists play in the healthcare system. It is also a tool for educators who seek to inspire and equip the next generation of pharmacists to uphold the highest standards of care and professionalism.

It is our hope that **"Textbook of Community Pharmacy: For Pharm.D"** will become an indispensable resource for students, educators, and practicing pharmacists, guiding them in their pursuit of excellence in community pharmacy practice. As the role of the pharmacist continues to evolve, we are confident that the knowledge and skills gained from this book will empower readers to make meaningful contributions to the health and well-being of their communities

Dr. Challa Srinivas Reddy
Dr. B.S. Sharvana Bhava
Dr. Santhi Sree Vemulapalli
Editor
Dr. Muralidhar Rao Akkaladevi

Textbook Of Community Pharmacy

For Pharm.D

ONE

INTRODUCTION TO COMMUNITY PHARMACY

Key Responsibilities of a Community Pharmacist

1.1 Definition of Community Pharmacy

Community pharmacy, a critical component of the healthcare system, refers to the practice of pharmacy in a community setting, primarily in retail pharmacies where pharmacists directly interact with patients. Unlike hospital or clinical pharmacy, which operates within healthcare institutions, community pharmacy is accessible to the general public and is often the first point of contact for individuals seeking healthcare services. This accessibility makes community pharmacy an essential link in the chain of healthcare delivery.

The definition of community pharmacy encompasses several aspects, including the provision of medicinal products, healthcare advice, and the promotion of health and well-being within the community. Pharmacists in community settings are responsible for dispensing medications prescribed by healthcare providers, ensuring that patients receive the correct dosage, and providing information on the safe and effective use of these medicines. This role extends beyond mere dispensing, as community pharmacists are increasingly involved in patient counseling, medication therapy management (MTM), and chronic disease management, making them pivotal in achieving optimal therapeutic outcomes.

In India, the role of community pharmacies is particularly significant due to the large population and the increasing burden of chronic diseases. Community pharmacists often act as the first point of consultation for minor ailments, offering advice on over-the-counter (OTC) medications and lifestyle modifications. This aspect of community pharmacy is crucial in rural and semi-urban areas where access to healthcare facilities may be limited. Community pharmacies also play a vital role in public health initiatives such as vaccination programs, health screenings, and educational campaigns aimed at preventing diseases.

Community pharmacy is also characterized by its involvement in the sale of OTC products, including vitamins, supplements, personal care items, and other health-related goods. This diversity of offerings enables community pharmacies to serve as a one-stop shop for many health and wellness needs, further enhancing their importance within the community. Moreover, community pharmacists are tasked with ensuring the quality, safety, and legality of the medicines they dispense, adhering to regulations and standards set by national and international bodies.

The evolving role of community pharmacy also includes a focus on preventive care, patient education, and collaboration with other healthcare professionals to ensure continuity of care. Pharmacists in the community setting are increasingly recognized for their expertise in medication management, particularly in managing polypharmacy among the elderly population, which is becoming more prevalent due to the rise in chronic conditions such as diabetes, hypertension, and cardiovascular diseases.

1.2 Scope of Community Pharmacy

The scope of community pharmacy is vast and continues to expand as the healthcare environment evolves. At its core, community pharmacy involves the provision of essential healthcare services, particularly in the management and dispensing of medications to the public. However, its role has grown beyond this fundamental function, encompassing a wide range of responsibilities that contribute to patient care, public health, and the overall improvement of health outcomes within the community.

One of the primary aspects of the scope of community pharmacy is the dispensing of prescription medications. Community pharmacists are responsible for ensuring that patients receive the correct medications as prescribed by their healthcare providers. This involves verifying prescriptions, checking for potential drug interactions, and educating patients on how to properly use their medications. The pharmacist's expertise is critical in preventing medication errors, which can have serious consequences for patient health.

In addition to dispensing medications, community pharmacies provide a broad array of over-the-counter (OTC) products, including analgesics, antipyretics, cough and cold remedies, vitamins, supplements, and personal care items. Pharmacists play a key role in advising patients on the appropriate use of these products, often serving as the first point of contact for individuals seeking relief from minor ailments. This aspect of community pharmacy is particularly important in areas where access to healthcare providers may be limited, as pharmacists can offer timely advice and treatment options.

The scope of community pharmacy also extends to patient counseling and education. Pharmacists are increasingly involved in medication therapy management (MTM), where they work with patients to optimize their medication regimens, particularly for those with chronic conditions such as diabetes, hypertension, and asthma. This role involves assessing the patient's medication use, identifying potential issues such as non-adherence or adverse effects, and providing tailored advice to improve therapeutic outcomes. By offering these services, community pharmacists help to bridge the gap between patients and healthcare providers, ensuring continuity of care and better health outcomes.

Another critical aspect of the scope of community pharmacy is its involvement in public health initiatives. Community pharmacies often participate in vaccination programs, offering immunizations for diseases such as influenza, COVID-19, hepatitis, and more. They also conduct health screenings for conditions like hypertension, diabetes, and hyperlipidemia, which are vital for early detection and management of these diseases. Furthermore, community pharmacists are involved in health promotion activities, such as smoking cessation programs and weight management counseling, which contribute to the prevention of chronic diseases.

Community pharmacies also play a crucial role in managing the healthcare needs of special populations, including the elderly, children, and individuals with multiple chronic conditions. For instance, pharmacists help manage polypharmacy in elderly patients by reviewing their medications to prevent adverse effects and ensuring that their treatment regimens are safe and effective. This aspect of community pharmacy is becoming increasingly important as the global population ages and the prevalence of chronic diseases rises.

In addition to these direct patient care activities, community pharmacists are also involved in the administrative and business aspects of pharmacy practice. This includes managing inventory, ensuring the availability of essential medications, complying with regulatory requirements, and maintaining accurate records. These responsibilities are vital for the smooth operation of the pharmacy and for ensuring that patients have consistent access to the medications and services they need.

The scope of community pharmacy is further expanding with the integration of digital health technologies. Telepharmacy, electronic health records (EHRs), and mobile health applications are transforming how pharmacists interact with patients and manage their health. These technologies enable pharmacists to provide remote consultations, monitor patient adherence, and offer personalized health advice, thereby extending the reach and impact of community pharmacy services.

1.3 Roles and Responsibilities of the Community Pharmacist

The roles and responsibilities of a community pharmacist are diverse and crucial to the effective delivery of healthcare services within the community. As highly trained healthcare professionals, community pharmacists are not only responsible for the safe dispensing of medications but also play a significant role in patient care, public health, and the management of healthcare resources. Their responsibilities extend across various domains, ensuring that they contribute to the overall well-being of the community they serve.

1.3.1 Patient Care

Patient care is at the heart of the community pharmacist's role, encompassing a wide range of activities aimed at improving the health and well-being of individuals within the community. The provision of patient care by pharmacists involves not only the dispensing of medications but also offering advice, managing treatment regimens, and ensuring that patients fully understand their medications and how to use them. This comprehensive approach to patient care helps in achieving better health outcomes and enhances the quality of life for patients.

One of the primary aspects of patient care in community pharmacy is **medication counseling**. Pharmacists provide essential information to patients about their prescribed medications, including how to take them correctly, possible side effects, and what to do in case of missed doses. This counseling is particularly important for patients with chronic conditions such as diabetes or hypertension, who may require long-term medication management. By offering clear and personalized advice, pharmacists help patients adhere to their medication regimens, which is crucial for the effectiveness of their treatment.

Medication therapy management (MTM) is another key component of patient care. This service involves a detailed review of the patient's medication regimen, with the pharmacist assessing the appropriateness, effectiveness, and safety of the prescribed drugs. MTM is particularly beneficial for patients with complex medical conditions or those taking multiple medications, as it helps to identify and resolve any issues such as drug interactions, side effects, or adherence problems. Through MTM, pharmacists can make recommendations to healthcare providers and work collaboratively to optimize the patient's therapy.

Community pharmacists also play a significant role in **disease prevention and health promotion**. They provide advice on lifestyle modifications, such as diet and exercise, which are essential for preventing and managing chronic diseases. Pharmacists often participate in public health campaigns, offering services such as smoking cessation programs, vaccination drives, and health screenings for conditions like hypertension and diabetes. By engaging in these activities, pharmacists contribute to the prevention of diseases and the promotion of healthier lifestyles within the community.

Patient education is a critical responsibility of community pharmacists. In addition to providing information about medications, pharmacists educate patients about their health conditions, the importance of adherence to treatment, and how to manage their symptoms effectively. This education empowers patients to take an active role in their health care, leading to better health outcomes. For instance, a patient with asthma may receive guidance on how to use inhalers properly, recognize triggers, and manage their condition effectively, reducing the risk of complications.

Another important aspect of patient care is **monitoring and follow-up**. Pharmacists often engage in follow-up consultations with patients, particularly those with chronic conditions, to monitor their progress and address any concerns or issues that may arise during treatment. This ongoing relationship between the pharmacist and patient ensures continuity of care and helps in early detection of potential problems, allowing for timely interventions. Regular follow-ups also provide an opportunity for pharmacists to adjust medication regimens as needed, based on the patient's response to treatment.

In summary, patient care in community pharmacy is a comprehensive and ongoing process that involves multiple facets of health management. By providing medication counseling, engaging in medication therapy management, promoting health and disease prevention, educating patients, and offering continuous monitoring and follow-up, community pharmacists play a pivotal role in ensuring the well-being of the individuals they serve. Their involvement in patient care not only enhances the effectiveness of treatment but also fosters a trusting relationship between the pharmacist and the patient, which is essential for achieving positive health outcomes.

1.3.2 Public Health

Community pharmacists play a crucial role in promoting public health, acting as accessible healthcare professionals who are often the first point of contact for individuals seeking medical advice. Their involvement in public health goes beyond dispensing medications; it includes active participation in health promotion, disease prevention, and the implementation of public health initiatives within the community. Through their work, pharmacists contribute significantly to improving the overall health and well-being of the population.

One of the key areas where community pharmacists contribute to public health is through **health education and promotion**. Pharmacists are uniquely positioned to educate the public on a wide range of health topics, from the importance of vaccinations to the management of chronic diseases like diabetes and hypertension. They provide personalized advice on lifestyle changes, such as healthy eating, regular exercise, and smoking cessation, which are essential for the prevention of many diseases. By raising awareness and offering practical guidance, pharmacists help individuals make informed decisions about their health, leading to better health outcomes.

Vaccination programs are another critical aspect of the pharmacist's role in public health. In many communities, pharmacists are authorized to administer vaccines, making them key players in immunization efforts.

They provide vaccines for influenza, COVID-19, hepatitis, and other preventable diseases, ensuring that more people have access to these vital services. The involvement of pharmacists in vaccination programs is particularly important in rural and underserved areas where access to other healthcare providers may be limited. By offering convenient and accessible vaccination services, pharmacists help to increase immunization rates, thereby reducing the spread of infectious diseases.

Community pharmacists also participate in **health screenings** for conditions such as hypertension, diabetes, and hyperlipidemia. These screenings are often offered as part of public health campaigns aimed at early detection and prevention of chronic diseases. By identifying individuals at risk, pharmacists can refer them to appropriate healthcare providers for further evaluation and treatment. Early detection through screening plays a crucial role in preventing the progression of diseases and reducing the overall burden on the healthcare system.

In addition to these activities, community pharmacists are involved in **managing public health emergencies**. During outbreaks of infectious diseases or other health crises, pharmacists are on the front lines, providing essential medications, information, and support to the community. Their knowledge and expertise make them invaluable in managing medication supplies, ensuring the availability of necessary treatments, and advising the public on preventive measures. For example, during the COVID-19 pandemic, pharmacists played a critical role in disseminating accurate information, providing vaccinations, and helping to manage the increased demand for healthcare services.

Community pharmacists also contribute to public health through their involvement in **disease prevention programs**. They offer services such as smoking cessation counseling, weight management programs, and advice on alcohol reduction, all of which are essential for preventing chronic diseases. By supporting patients in making healthier lifestyle choices, pharmacists help to reduce the incidence of conditions such as cardiovascular disease, diabetes, and cancer, ultimately improving the health of the community.

Moreover, community pharmacists engage in **collaboration with other healthcare professionals** to enhance public health outcomes. They work alongside doctors, nurses, and public health officials to implement health promotion activities, manage chronic diseases, and address public health challenges. This collaborative approach ensures that patients receive comprehensive care and that public health initiatives are more effective in reaching their goals.

Activity	Description	Examples
Health Education and Promotion	Providing information and guidance on health topics to the community.	Educational campaigns on vaccination, diet, exercise.
Disease Prevention	Engaging in activities that prevent the onset of chronic diseases.	Counseling on smoking cessation, blood pressure monitoring.
Vaccination Programs	Administering vaccines and promoting immunization within the community.	Flu shots, COVID-19 vaccines, Hepatitis B vaccination.
Health Screenings	Conducting screenings for early detection of chronic diseases.	Blood pressure checks, diabetes screening, cholesterol testing.
Public Health Campaigns	Participating in or leading public health initiatives to raise awareness and promote health.	Campaigns on the dangers of smoking, healthy living workshops.
Emergency Response	Providing support and services during public health emergencies.	Distributing medications during outbreaks, providing health information.
Collaboration with Healthcare Providers	Working with other healthcare professionals to enhance public health outcomes.	Coordinating care with doctors, participating in public health planning.

Key roles and activities that community pharmacists perform in promoting public health:

1.3.3 Medication Management

Medication management is a central responsibility of the community pharmacist, encompassing a range of activities aimed at ensuring that patients use their medications safely, effectively, and appropriately. Effective medication management is critical for optimizing therapeutic outcomes, reducing the risk of adverse effects, and improving patient adherence to prescribed treatment regimens. Community pharmacists, with their expertise in pharmacology and patient care, are uniquely positioned to oversee and manage medication use in the community setting.

At the core of medication management is the process of **medication reconciliation**. This involves reviewing a patient's complete medication list, including prescription medications, over-the-counter drugs, and supplements, to identify and resolve any potential conflicts or interactions. Pharmacists ensure that the medications are appropriate for the patient's condition, check for any duplications or omissions, and verify that the dosages are correct. This process is especially important for patients who are transitioning between different levels of care, such as from hospital to home, where there is a higher risk of medication errors.

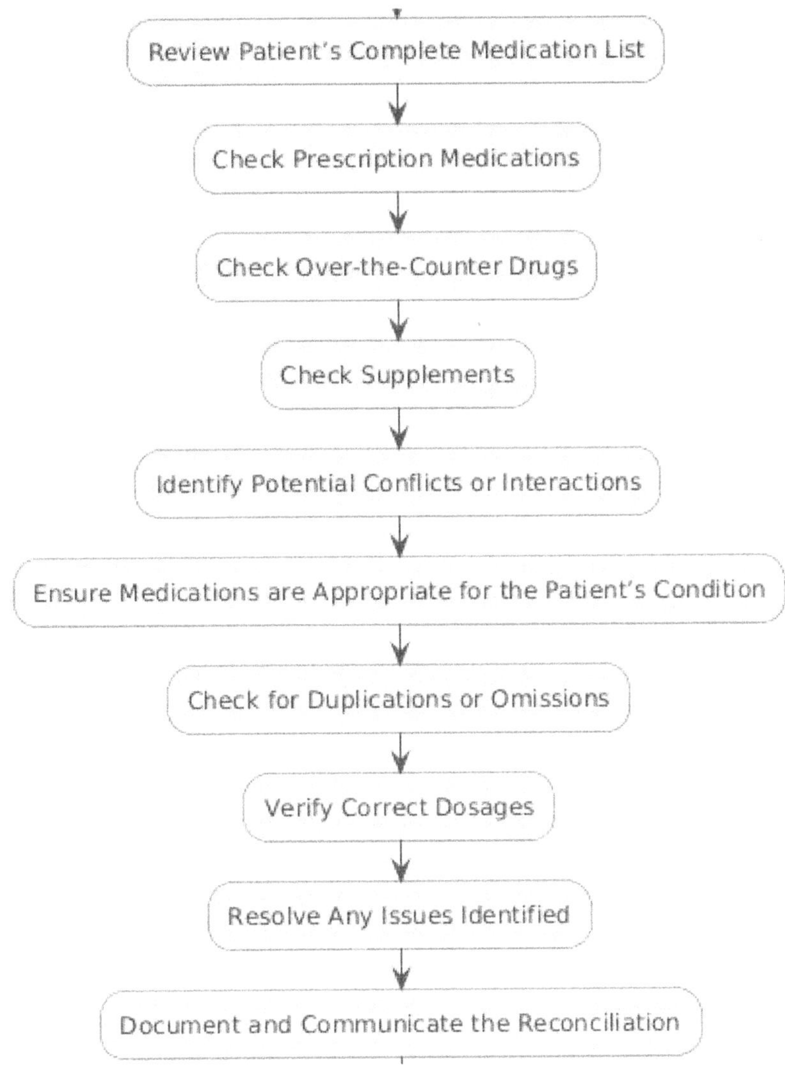

Fowchart for the Medication Reconciliation process

Patient counseling and education form another critical aspect of medication management. Pharmacists provide detailed explanations to patients about how to take their medications, the importance of adherence, and what to do if they miss a dose. They also educate patients about potential side effects and how to manage them. By providing this information, pharmacists empower patients to take an active role in their treatment, which can lead to better health outcomes and greater satisfaction with care. For example, a patient with diabetes might receive counseling on how to properly administer insulin and monitor blood glucose levels, which is essential for effective diabetes management.

Another key component of medication management is **medication therapy management (MTM)**, a service that involves a comprehensive review of all medications a patient is taking. During an MTM session, the pharmacist assesses the efficacy and safety of each medication, identifies any problems, and develops a plan to resolve them. This service is particularly valuable for patients with chronic conditions who may be on complex medication regimens. By optimizing medication use, pharmacists help to improve therapeutic outcomes, reduce the likelihood of adverse drug events, and enhance the overall quality of life for patients.

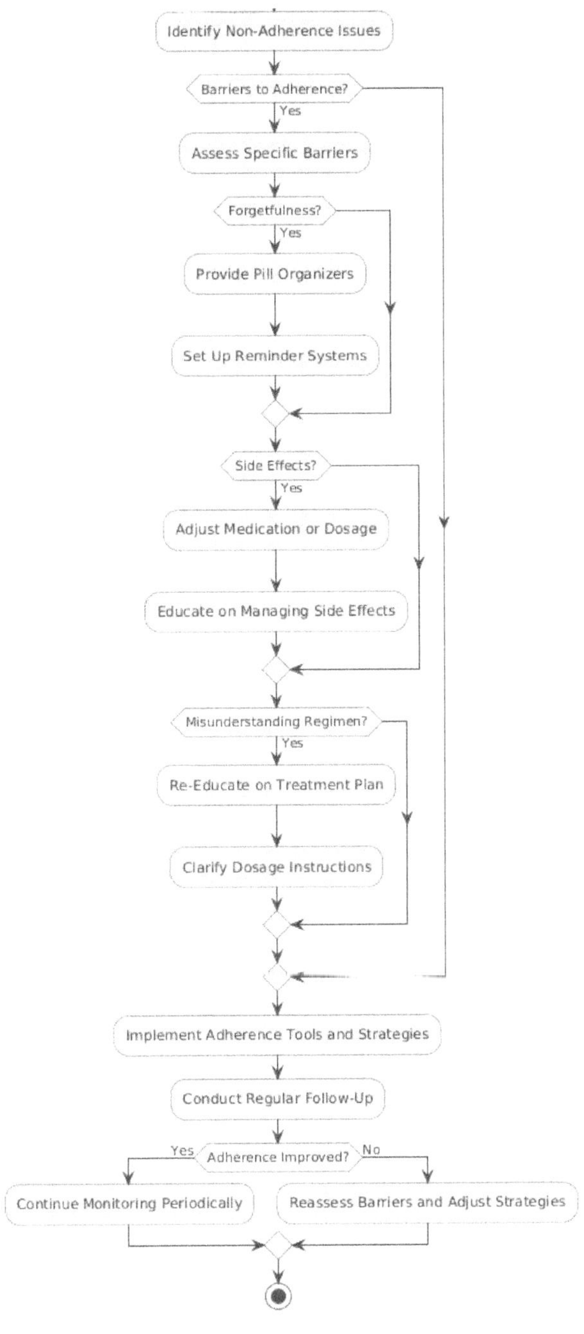

Flowchart that outlines the Medication Therapy Management process

Adherence monitoring is also an important responsibility in medication management. Non-adherence to prescribed medications is a common issue that can lead to treatment failure, worsening of the condition, and increased healthcare costs. Pharmacists play a vital role in identifying barriers to adherence, such as forgetfulness, side effects, or misunderstanding of the treatment regimen. They work with patients to overcome these barriers, providing tools and strategies, such as pill organizers or reminder systems, to help patients take their medications as prescribed. Regular follow-up and monitoring allow pharmacists to make adjustments as needed, ensuring that patients remain on track with their treatment.

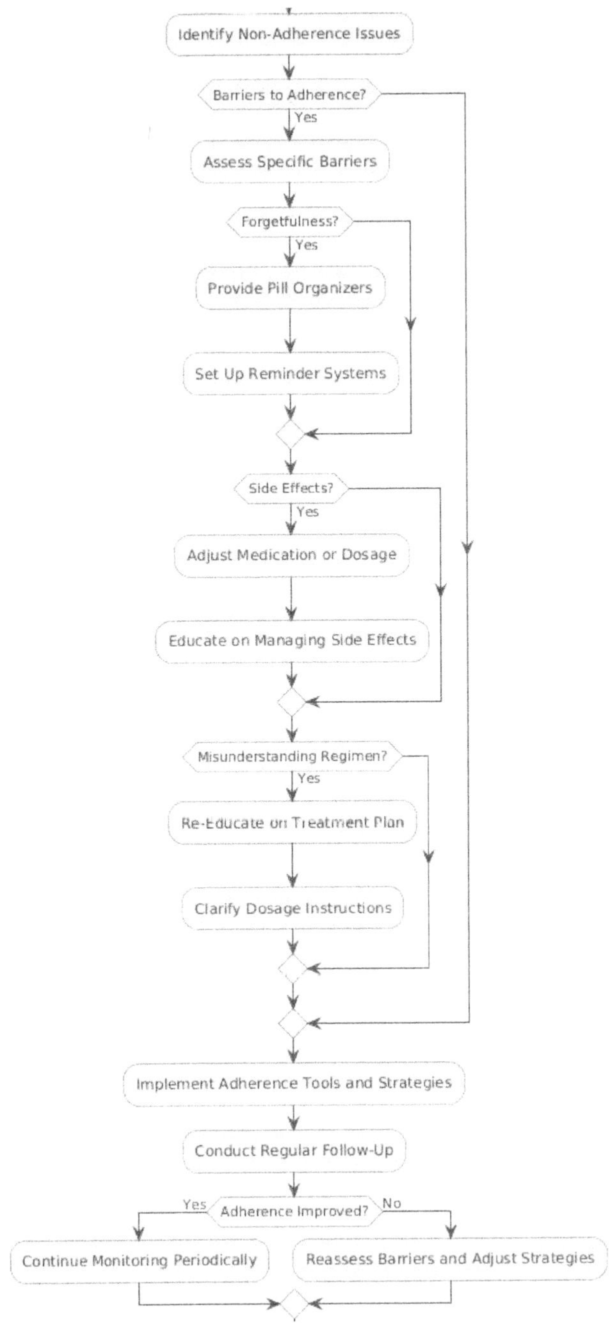

Adherence Monitoring Process in Medication Management

Managing polypharmacy—the use of multiple medications by a patient, especially common among the elderly—is another significant aspect of medication management. Polypharmacy increases the risk of drug interactions, adverse effects, and medication non-adherence. Pharmacists carefully review the medication regimens of patients on multiple drugs, looking for opportunities to simplify the regimen, discontinue unnecessary medications, or switch to safer alternatives. This process not only reduces the potential for harm but also enhances the patient's ability to adhere to their treatment plan.

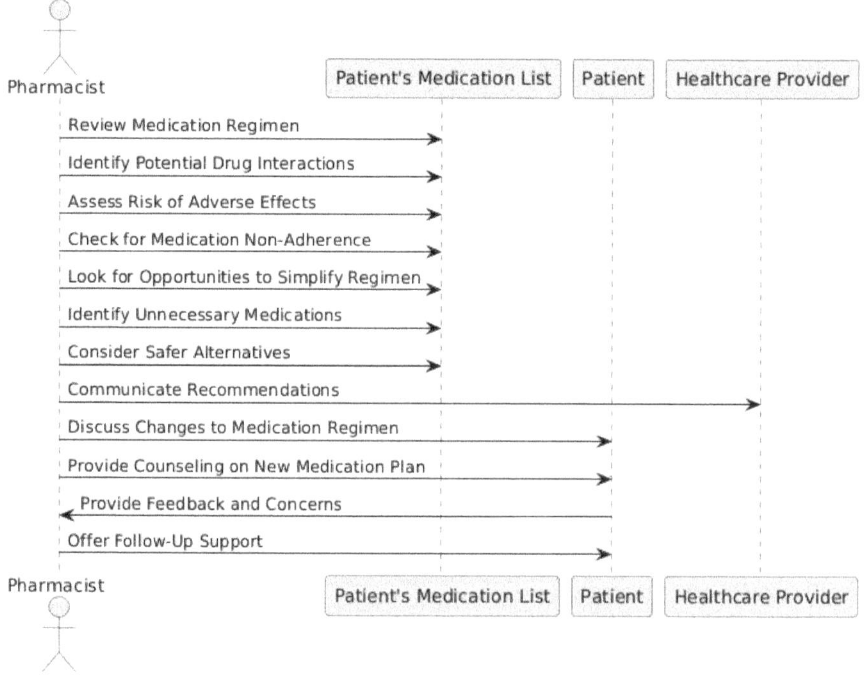

Managing Polypharmacy

In addition to these direct patient care activities, pharmacists are involved in **ensuring medication safety** through the proper storage, handling, and dispensing of medications. They must comply with regulations regarding the storage conditions of drugs, ensuring that medications are kept at the appropriate temperature and are protected from light or moisture, as required. Pharmacists also ensure that medications are dispensed in the correct packaging and with appropriate labeling to prevent errors and ensure that patients understand how to use their medications correctly.

Collaboration with other healthcare providers is also a key element of medication management. Pharmacists work closely with doctors, nurses, and other healthcare professionals to coordinate care and ensure that all aspects of the patient's treatment are aligned. This collaboration is essential for managing complex cases where multiple providers are involved, as it helps to avoid duplication of therapy, ensures consistency in care, and enhances the overall effectiveness of the treatment plan.

1.3.4 Health Promotion and Education

Health promotion and education are fundamental responsibilities of the community pharmacist, playing a critical role in enhancing public health and preventing diseases. Community pharmacists are uniquely positioned to provide health education and promote healthy lifestyles due to their accessibility and frequent interactions with patients. By delivering accurate and relevant health information, pharmacists empower individuals to make informed decisions about their health, contributing to better health outcomes and reducing the burden of chronic diseases.

One of the primary aspects of health promotion in community pharmacy is **disease prevention**. Pharmacists engage in activities aimed at preventing the onset of chronic diseases such as diabetes, hypertension, and cardiovascular diseases. They provide advice on lifestyle modifications that are crucial for disease prevention, including recommendations on diet, physical activity, and smoking cessation. For instance, a pharmacist might counsel a patient on reducing salt intake to manage blood pressure or offer tips on incorporating more physical activity into their daily routine to prevent obesity-related conditions. By promoting these healthy behaviors, pharmacists help reduce the incidence of chronic diseases within the community.

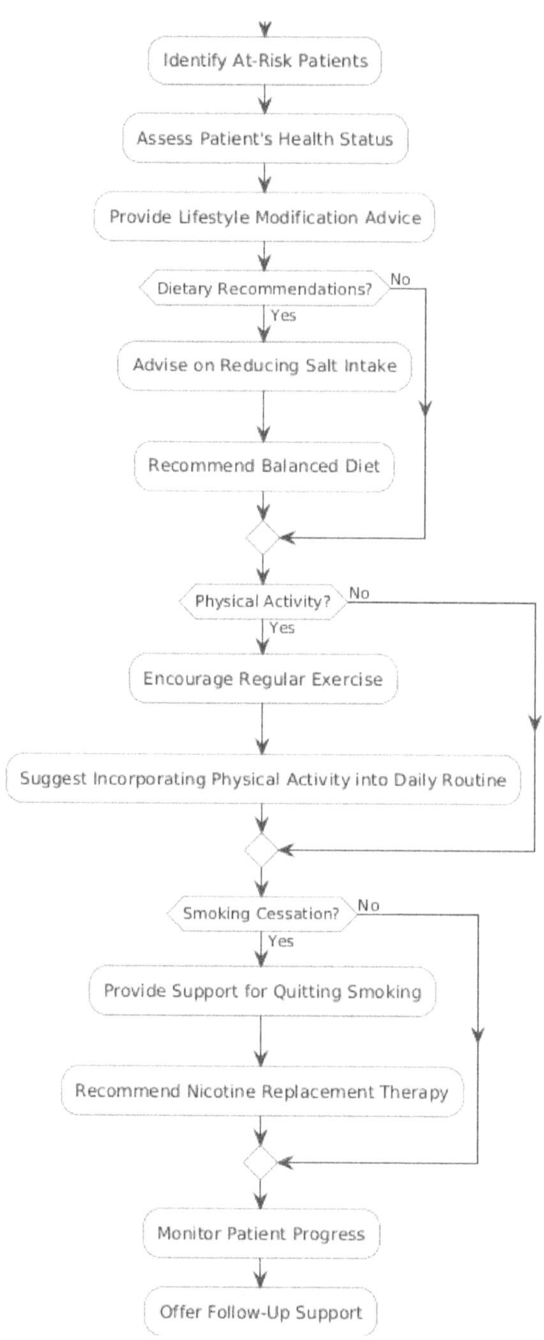

Flowchart - the Disease Prevention activities in community pharmacy:

Patient education is another vital component of health promotion. Pharmacists educate patients on a wide range of health topics, including the importance of medication adherence, understanding medical conditions, and recognizing the early signs of illness. For example, a pharmacist might explain the symptoms of high blood sugar to a patient at risk of diabetes, or they might educate a patient with asthma on how to avoid triggers and properly use an inhaler. This education is particularly important for patients with chronic conditions, as it helps them manage their health more effectively and avoid complications.

Community pharmacists also play a significant role in **public health campaigns**. They often participate in or lead initiatives aimed at raising awareness about public health issues such as vaccination, smoking cessation, and the risks of alcohol abuse. These campaigns may involve distributing educational materials, organizing health talks, or providing screenings and consultations. For example, during flu season, pharmacists might actively promote influenza vaccinations, providing information about the benefits of getting vaccinated and addressing common misconceptions. By engaging in these activities, pharmacists contribute to the overall health literacy of the community and encourage preventive care.

Health screenings conducted by pharmacists are an essential aspect of health promotion. These screenings help identify individuals at risk of developing chronic conditions or those who may already have undiagnosed conditions. For instance, pharmacists may offer blood pressure checks, cholesterol testing, or blood glucose monitoring. Early detection through these screenings allows for timely intervention, which can prevent the progression of diseases and reduce the need for more intensive medical treatments. Pharmacists often provide follow-up advice and referrals to healthcare providers based on the results of these screenings, ensuring that patients receive the care they need.

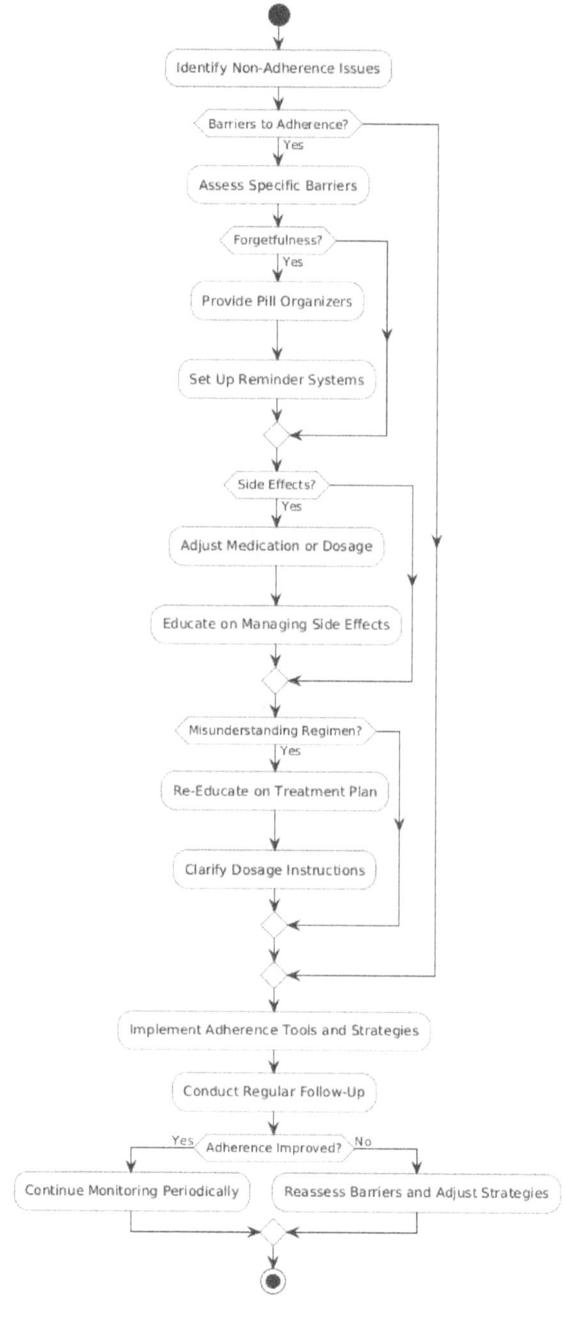
Identify Non-Adherence Issues
Barriers to Adherence?
Yes
Assess Specific Barriers
Forgetfulness?
Yes
Provide Pill Organizers
Set Up Reminder Systems
Side Effects?
Yes
Adjust Medication or Dosage
Educate on Managing Side Effects
Misunderstanding Regimen?
Yes
Re-Educate on Treatment Plan
Clarify Dosage Instructions
Implement Adherence Tools and Strategies
Conduct Regular Follow-Up
Yes
Adherence Improved?
No
Continue Monitoring Periodically
Reassess Barriers and Adjust Strategies

In addition to direct patient interactions, pharmacists contribute to health promotion through **collaboration with other healthcare professionals**. By working with doctors, nurses, and public health officials, pharmacists help coordinate care and reinforce health messages. This collaboration ensures that patients receive consistent information and support from all members of their healthcare team, which enhances the effectiveness of health promotion efforts. For example, a pharmacist might collaborate with a local clinic to run a joint smoking cessation program, providing both medication support and counseling to participants.

The role of the community pharmacist in health promotion and education is further expanded by the increasing use of **digital health tools**. Pharmacists can leverage technology to reach a broader audience, offering online consultations, educational webinars, and mobile apps that track health metrics. These tools allow pharmacists to provide continuous support and education to patients, even when they are not physically present in the pharmacy. By integrating digital health solutions into their practice, pharmacists can enhance their reach and impact, making health promotion more accessible and personalized.

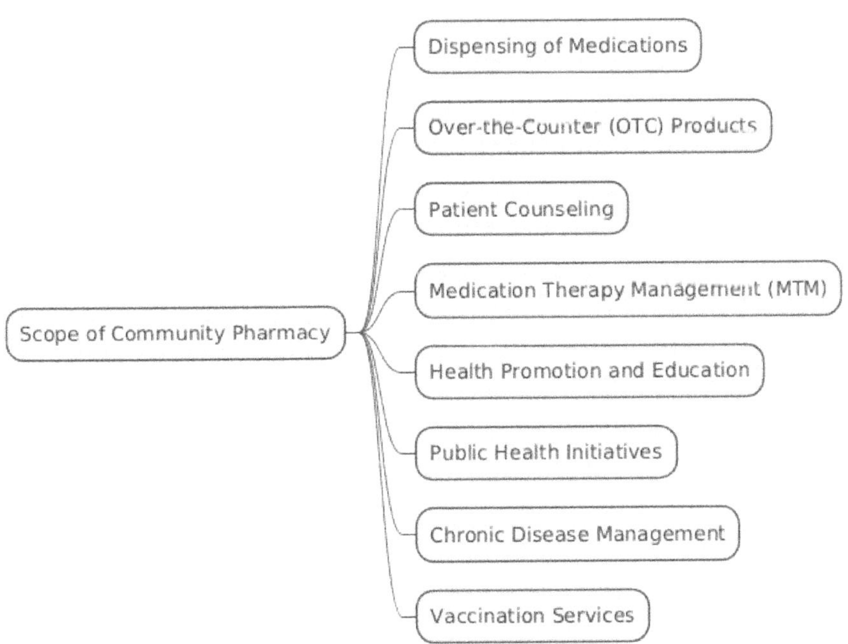

TWO

Community Pharmacy Management

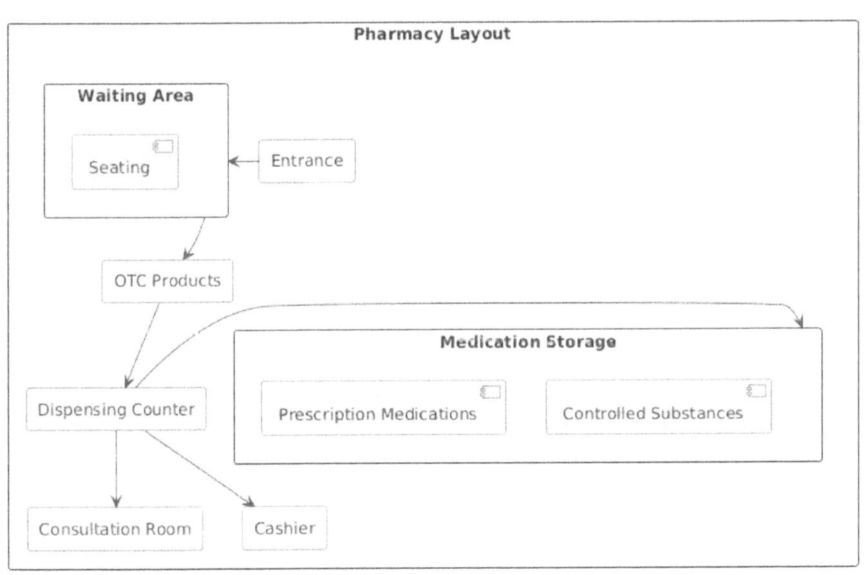

Pharmacy Layout

2.1 Site Selection and Space Layout

2.1.1 Criteria for Site Selection

Selecting the appropriate site for a community pharmacy is one of the most critical decisions that can influence the success and sustainability of the business. The location of a pharmacy directly impacts its accessibility to customers, visibility in the community, and ultimately, its profitability. Therefore, a thorough analysis of various criteria is essential before finalizing the site.

One of the primary criteria for site selection is demographic analysis. Understanding the population characteristics of the area is crucial. A community with a higher proportion of elderly residents may demand more prescription medications and chronic disease management services. Conversely, an area with a younger population might require more over-the-counter (OTC) products, wellness products, and contraceptives. Evaluating the population size, age distribution, and income levels can help determine the potential demand for pharmacy services in that area. Additionally, it is important to consider the cultural and ethnic composition of the community, as this can influence the types of products and services that will be in demand.

Another important criterion is the proximity to healthcare providers. Pharmacies located near hospitals, clinics, or doctors' offices often experience higher foot traffic, as patients prefer to fill their prescriptions immediately after a medical consultation. The convenience of having a pharmacy nearby can encourage repeat business and foster strong relationships with healthcare providers, who may refer patients to the pharmacy for their medication needs. In addition, being close to healthcare providers allows for better collaboration in patient care, which can enhance the pharmacy's reputation in the community.

Competition analysis is also a vital factor in site selection. It is important to assess the number and type of existing pharmacies in the area. A location with few competitors might seem advantageous, but it is essential to consider whether the local market can sustain another pharmacy. On the other hand, setting up a pharmacy in an area with numerous competitors might require a differentiation strategy, such as offering specialized services or extended hours, to attract customers. Analyzing the services and products offered by competitors can help identify gaps in the market that the new pharmacy can fill.

Accessibility and visibility of the site are other key considerations. The pharmacy should be easily accessible by foot, car, and public transportation. Ample parking space is essential for customers who drive, while proximity to bus stops or metro stations can attract those who rely on public transport. The site should also have high visibility, as this can significantly enhance the pharmacy's brand presence. Locations on busy streets, near shopping centers, or in commercial districts are often ideal, as they attract a steady flow of potential customers. Signage and storefront design also play a crucial role in making the pharmacy noticeable to passersby.

Economic and regulatory factors must also be taken into account. The cost of leasing or purchasing the property is a significant investment, and it should align with the expected revenue from the pharmacy's operations. It is also essential to consider the long-term sustainability of the location, including any potential for growth or development in the area that could impact the pharmacy's business. Additionally, the site must comply with all local zoning laws and regulations regarding the operation of a pharmacy. This includes ensuring that the premises meet the necessary health and safety standards, as well as obtaining the required licenses and permits from local authorities.

Lastly, community needs and preferences should guide the site selection process. Engaging with the community to understand their needs and preferences can provide valuable insights. For example, if there is a strong demand for home delivery services or extended hours, the pharmacy can tailor its offerings accordingly. Understanding the specific health concerns of the community, such as a high prevalence of diabetes or cardiovascular diseases, can also help the pharmacy to stock relevant medications and offer targeted health services.

Criteria	Description	Considerations
Demographic Analysis	Understanding the population characteristics of the area.	Population size, age distribution, income levels, cultural and ethnic composition.
Proximity to Healthcare Providers	Location near hospitals, clinics, or doctors' offices.	Increased foot traffic, collaboration with healthcare providers, convenience for patients.
Competition Analysis	Evaluating the number and type of existing pharmacies in the area.	Number of competitors, services offered by competitors, market saturation, differentiation strategies.
Accessibility and Visibility	Ensuring the pharmacy is easily accessible and visible to potential customers.	Accessibility by foot, car, public transportation, ample parking, location on busy streets or commercial areas.
Economic and Regulatory Factors	Assessing the financial and legal aspects of the site.	Cost of leasing/purchasing, potential for growth, compliance with zoning laws, health and safety standards.
Community Needs and Preferences	Aligning with the specific needs and preferences of the community.	Demand for services like home delivery, extended hours, specific health concerns (e.g., diabetes management).

Key criteria for site selection in community pharmacy

2.1.2 Design and Layout of the Pharmacy Space

The design and layout of a community pharmacy are crucial elements that significantly influence the efficiency of operations, the satisfaction of customers, and the overall success of the business. A well-thought-out pharmacy layout can enhance workflow, improve customer experience, and ensure that the pharmacy complies with regulatory standards. Therefore, careful planning is essential when designing the physical space of the pharmacy.

One of the most important aspects of pharmacy design is the **workflow efficiency**. The layout should facilitate the smooth movement of staff and customers within the pharmacy. This involves strategically placing key areas such as the dispensing counter, storage areas, and consultation rooms to minimize unnecessary movement and reduce the time taken to fulfill prescriptions. For instance, the dispensing area should be centrally located to allow quick access to medication stock and easy communication with customers. The workflow should also consider the privacy needs of customers, particularly in areas where sensitive information is discussed, such as consultation rooms or the prescription drop-off counter.

Another critical factor in the design and layout is **customer accessibility and comfort**. The pharmacy space should be welcoming and easy to navigate, ensuring that customers can find what they need without difficulty. Wide aisles, clear signage, and well-organized shelving can help customers move through the pharmacy with ease. The layout should also accommodate customers with disabilities, ensuring compliance with accessibility standards. This includes features such as ramps, wide doorways, and lower counters to accommodate wheelchairs. Additionally, providing seating areas for customers who may need to wait for their prescriptions can enhance comfort and satisfaction.

Safety and security are also paramount in the design of a pharmacy. The layout must ensure that medications are stored securely and that sensitive areas, such as the controlled substances storage, are accessible only to authorized personnel. The design should include secure storage solutions, such as lockable cabinets and safes, to prevent unauthorized access to medications. Furthermore, the layout should facilitate easy supervision of the entire pharmacy space to deter theft and ensure that staff can quickly respond to any security concerns. The placement of security cameras and alarm systems should be considered as part of the overall design to enhance safety.

Compliance with regulatory standards is another essential consideration in pharmacy design. The layout must adhere to local health and safety regulations, which may include requirements for ventilation, lighting, and hygiene. For example, adequate lighting is necessary not only for customer comfort but also to ensure that pharmacists can accurately read prescriptions and labels. Ventilation systems should be designed to maintain a clean and safe environment, particularly in areas where medications are prepared or stored. Hygiene is another critical factor, and the layout should include easy-to-clean surfaces and areas designated for handwashing to prevent contamination.

The design should also take into account the **future growth and adaptability** of the pharmacy. As the business grows, the pharmacy may need to expand its services, such as adding a vaccination room or increasing storage space for medications. Therefore, the initial design should be flexible enough to accommodate future changes without requiring a complete overhaul. This might include modular furniture that can be easily reconfigured, or the inclusion of extra storage areas that can be utilized as the need arises.

In terms of **aesthetic appeal**, the design and layout of the pharmacy should reflect the brand's image and create a positive first impression for customers. A clean, modern, and well-maintained space can enhance the customer experience and build trust in the pharmacy's services. The use of colors, lighting, and materials should be carefully considered to create a welcoming environment. For instance, calming colors and natural lighting can make the space feel more comfortable and inviting, encouraging customers to spend more time in the pharmacy.

2.2.1 Recruitment and Training

Recruitment and training are fundamental components of staff management in community pharmacy. The success of a pharmacy largely depends on the quality and competence of its staff, making the recruitment process critical. It is essential to attract and select individuals who not only have the necessary qualifications and skills but also possess the right attitude and commitment to providing excellent patient care. The recruitment process typically involves several stages, including job analysis, advertising, screening, interviewing, and selecting the right candidates.

Job analysis is the first step in recruitment, where the roles and responsibilities of the position are clearly defined. This involves determining the specific tasks that the employee will be responsible for, the qualifications required, and the competencies that are necessary for success in the role. For example, a pharmacy technician must have a solid understanding of pharmaceutical practices, attention to detail, and excellent communication skills. Once the job description is finalized, the next step is to advertise the position.

Advertising the position is crucial to attract a pool of suitable candidates. This can be done through various channels, including online job portals, professional networks, and local newspapers. The advertisement should be clear and concise, outlining the key responsibilities, qualifications, and expectations for the role. Additionally, the advertisement should reflect the pharmacy's values and culture to attract candidates who align with the organization's ethos. For example, if the pharmacy places a high value on customer service, this should be emphasized in the job ad to attract candidates who are customer-focused.

Screening and interviewing candidates are the next steps in the recruitment process. Screening involves reviewing resumes and applications to shortlist candidates who meet the required qualifications and experience. This process helps to filter out unsuitable candidates early on, saving time and resources. Once the shortlist is created, the selected candidates are invited for interviews. The interview process is critical as it provides an opportunity to assess the candidate's suitability for the role, including their technical knowledge, problem-solving abilities, and interpersonal skills. It is important to ask open-ended questions that allow candidates to demonstrate their competence and fit for the role. For example, a candidate might be asked how they would handle a difficult customer situation or how they ensure accuracy when dispensing medications.

After selecting the right candidate, **training** becomes a key focus. Effective training is essential to ensure that new employees are fully equipped to perform their duties and contribute to the success of the pharmacy. Training should be comprehensive and cover all aspects of the job, including understanding the pharmacy's procedures, learning about the medications and products offered, and familiarizing themselves with the technology used in the pharmacy, such as dispensing software. For example, a newly hired pharmacy technician should receive training on how to use the pharmacy management system, including entering prescriptions, managing inventory, and processing payments.

On-the-job training is particularly important in a community pharmacy setting. This type of training allows new employees to learn by doing, under the supervision of experienced staff members. It provides hands-on experience and helps to build confidence in performing tasks. Additionally, regular feedback during the training process is crucial for the development of the employee. Constructive feedback helps employees understand what they are doing well and where they need to improve, enabling them to grow in their role.

Ongoing training and professional development are also vital components of staff management. The pharmacy industry is constantly evolving, with new medications, technologies, and regulations emerging regularly. It is important for staff to stay updated with these changes to provide the best possible care to patients. This can be achieved through regular training sessions, attending workshops, and participating in continuing education programs. For example, pharmacists might attend a workshop on the latest developments in diabetes management or participate in an online course about new pharmaceutical regulations.

2.2.2 Roles and Responsibilities of Pharmacy Staff

The roles and responsibilities of pharmacy staff are critical in ensuring the smooth operation of the pharmacy and the delivery of high-quality care to patients. Each member of the pharmacy team has specific duties that contribute to the overall functioning of the pharmacy, and understanding these roles is essential for effective management. The pharmacy team typically includes pharmacists, pharmacy technicians, pharmacy assistants, and sometimes administrative staff, each playing a vital role in the daily operations.

Pharmacists are the healthcare professionals responsible for overseeing the entire pharmacy operation. Their primary role is to ensure that medications are dispensed accurately and safely to patients. Pharmacists review prescriptions for accuracy, check for potential drug interactions, and provide counseling to patients on the proper use of their medications. They also play a key role in patient education, offering advice on managing chronic conditions, such as diabetes or hypertension, and answering any questions patients may have about their medications. Additionally, pharmacists are responsible for maintaining records of all prescriptions dispensed and ensuring that the pharmacy complies with all regulatory requirements, including those related to controlled substances. For example, a pharmacist may need to verify the identity of a patient before dispensing a controlled medication and ensure that all records are meticulously maintained to comply with legal standards.

Pharmacy technicians assist pharmacists in the preparation and dispensing of medications. They are often responsible for tasks such as counting and labeling medications, preparing prescription orders, and managing inventory. Pharmacy technicians also play a crucial role in maintaining the accuracy of the pharmacy's operations by ensuring that all medications are correctly labeled and stored according to regulatory standards. In many cases, pharmacy technicians are also involved in compounding medications, which involves preparing specific doses or forms of medication as prescribed by a healthcare provider. For instance, they may be required to prepare a liquid formulation of a medication for a child who cannot swallow pills. Moreover, pharmacy technicians often assist with administrative tasks, such as processing insurance claims and managing the pharmacy's inventory, ensuring that all necessary medications are in stock and readily available.

Pharmacy assistants typically perform support tasks that help to keep the pharmacy running smoothly. Their responsibilities often include managing the front end of the pharmacy, such as handling customer service, answering phones, and ringing up sales. Pharmacy assistants may also assist in the stocking of shelves, organizing products, and ensuring that the pharmacy remains clean and well-organized. While they do not dispense medications, pharmacy assistants play an important role in supporting the pharmacists and technicians by managing the non-clinical aspects of the pharmacy's operations. For example, a pharmacy assistant might help a customer find an over-the-counter product, answer questions about store hours, or assist with the packaging of medications for delivery.

Administrative staff, when present, are responsible for the back-office operations of the pharmacy. Their duties can include managing the pharmacy's finances, handling payroll, ordering supplies, and ensuring that all administrative functions are running efficiently. While they may not be directly involved in patient care, their work is essential to the overall success of the pharmacy. Administrative staff help to ensure that the pharmacy operates smoothly from a business perspective, allowing pharmacists and technicians to focus on patient care. For example, an administrative assistant might be responsible for managing the pharmacy's billing processes, ensuring that all invoices are accurate and submitted on time.

In addition to these defined roles, all pharmacy staff share the responsibility of ensuring a positive experience for patients and customers. This includes maintaining a professional and welcoming environment, addressing customer concerns promptly, and working together as a team to meet the needs of the community. Effective communication and collaboration among the pharmacy staff are essential for providing high-quality care and ensuring the efficient operation of the pharmacy. For instance, clear communication between pharmacists and technicians is critical when handling complex prescriptions or when there is a need for clarification on a prescription order.

2.3.1 Coding and Stocking of Medications

The coding and stocking of medications are vital components of materials management in a community pharmacy. Proper management of medication inventory ensures that the pharmacy operates efficiently, minimizes waste, and meets the needs of patients consistently. The processes involved in coding and stocking are designed to maintain accurate inventory records, ensure the correct storage of medications, and facilitate quick and accurate dispensing by pharmacy staff.

Coding of medications is the first step in organizing the pharmacy's inventory. Each medication is assigned a unique code or identifier, which helps in tracking and managing the stock. This code typically includes information such as the medication's name, dosage form, strength, and expiration date. The coding system allows for easy identification of medications, both in the storage area and within the pharmacy's inventory management software. For example, a bottle of amoxicillin 500 mg capsules might be coded as AMX500CAP, with additional identifiers for batch number and expiration date. This system ensures that medications are easily distinguishable from one another, reducing the risk of errors during dispensing.

In addition to providing a systematic way to organize medications, coding also plays a crucial role in **inventory management**. Pharmacy staff can quickly check the inventory status of a particular medication using its code, enabling them to reorder stock before it runs out. This is particularly important for high-demand medications that need to be readily available to meet patient needs. Moreover, coding facilitates the monitoring of medication expiration dates. By incorporating expiration dates into the coding system, pharmacy staff can prioritize the use of medications that are closest to their expiration, thereby reducing waste and ensuring that patients receive fresh, effective medications.

Stocking of medications involves the physical placement of medications in the pharmacy's storage area. Proper stocking is essential for maintaining an organized and efficient pharmacy. Medications should be stored in a manner that ensures their safety, effectiveness, and accessibility. This includes following guidelines for temperature control, humidity, and light exposure, as some medications require specific conditions to remain stable. For instance, refrigerated medications such as certain vaccines and insulin should be stored in designated refrigeration units at controlled temperatures. Similarly, medications sensitive to light should be stored in opaque containers or areas shielded from direct light.

The **organization of the storage area** is another critical aspect of stocking medications. Medications should be arranged logically, typically by therapeutic category, dosage form, or alphabetically by brand or generic name. This organization allows pharmacy staff to quickly locate and retrieve medications when filling prescriptions. For example, all antihypertensive medications might be stored in one section, while antibiotics are stored in another. Within each section, medications can be further organized by dosage form, such as tablets, capsules, or liquids, and by strength. This systematic arrangement reduces the time spent searching for medications, thereby improving the efficiency of the pharmacy.

Stock rotation is an important practice in the stocking process. This involves placing newer stock behind older stock on the shelves to ensure that the older stock is used first. This "first-in, first-out" (FIFO) method helps prevent medications from expiring before they are used. Regular stock checks should be conducted to identify and remove expired or nearly expired medications from the shelves. This practice not only minimizes waste but also ensures patient safety by preventing the dispensing of expired medications.

Barcode scanning systems are increasingly used in modern pharmacies to enhance the accuracy and efficiency of the coding and stocking process. Each medication is labeled with a barcode that corresponds to its code in the pharmacy's inventory system. When stocking medications, pharmacy staff can scan the barcode to automatically update the inventory records. This reduces the likelihood of human error and ensures that the inventory data is always up-to-date. Additionally, barcode scanning can be used during the dispensing process to verify that the correct medication is being provided to the patient, further enhancing safety.

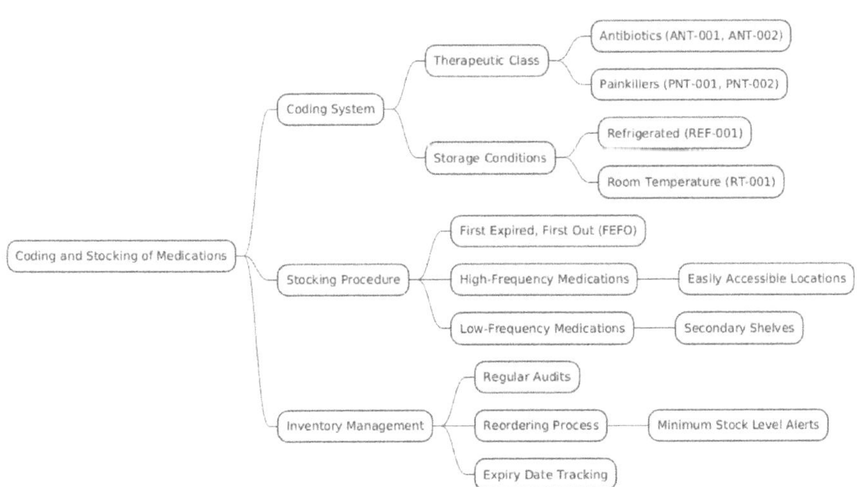

2.3.2 Inventory Management and Reordering

Inventory management and reordering are critical functions in the daily operations of a community pharmacy. Effective inventory management ensures that the pharmacy maintains an adequate supply of medications to meet patient needs while minimizing waste and reducing carrying costs. A well-organized inventory system allows the pharmacy to track stock levels, manage expiration dates, and anticipate future needs, all of which contribute to the smooth running of the business.

Inventory management begins with the accurate tracking of stock levels. This involves maintaining detailed records of all medications and products in the pharmacy, including their quantities, locations, and expiration dates. Many pharmacies use computerized inventory management systems to automate this process, which reduces the risk of human error and allows for real-time updates. For example, when a medication is dispensed, the system automatically deducts the corresponding amount from the inventory, ensuring that the stock levels are always current. This system also allows for easy retrieval of information regarding a specific medication, such as its expiration date or batch number, which is crucial for ensuring that patients receive safe and effective medications.

Regular inventory audits are an essential part of inventory management. These audits involve physically counting the stock on hand and comparing it to the inventory records to identify any discrepancies. Such discrepancies can occur due to various reasons, including theft, loss, or administrative errors. Regular audits help to detect these issues early, allowing the pharmacy to take corrective action promptly. For instance, if a significant discrepancy is found in the stock of a high-cost medication, the pharmacy might investigate to determine if there was a mistake in the dispensing process or if theft is suspected. Audits also provide an opportunity to identify slow-moving stock that may need to be discounted or returned to the supplier to avoid expiration.

Reordering is the process of replenishing the pharmacy's stock to maintain adequate levels of all medications. Effective reordering requires careful planning and monitoring of stock levels to avoid both stockouts and overstocking. Stockouts can lead to a situation where the pharmacy is unable to fulfill prescriptions, which can negatively impact patient care and the pharmacy's reputation. On the other hand, overstocking ties up capital in unsold inventory and increases the risk of medications expiring before they can be used. Therefore, pharmacies typically set minimum and maximum stock levels for each medication, known as reorder points. When the stock level of a particular medication falls to its reorder point, the system generates an alert or automatically places an order with the supplier.

Supplier management is also a crucial aspect of reordering. Building strong relationships with reliable suppliers ensures that the pharmacy receives its orders on time and at competitive prices. It is important to work with suppliers who can provide consistent quality, offer favorable payment terms, and respond quickly to urgent requests. For instance, if there is a sudden increase in demand for a particular medication due to a local outbreak of illness, a responsive supplier can ensure that the pharmacy receives additional stock quickly. Additionally, pharmacies should consider diversifying their suppliers to reduce the risk of supply chain disruptions.

Automated reordering systems are increasingly used in modern pharmacies to streamline the reordering process. These systems can be set up to automatically place orders based on predefined reorder points and usage patterns. For example, if the inventory management system detects that the stock of a commonly prescribed medication is nearing its minimum level, it can automatically generate and send a purchase order to the supplier. This not only saves time but also reduces the risk of human error in the reordering process. Automated systems can also help pharmacies take advantage of bulk purchasing discounts by aggregating orders for multiple items from the same supplier.

Handling of backorders and shortages is another important aspect of inventory management. Sometimes, suppliers may not be able to fulfill an order due to shortages or manufacturing delays, resulting in a backorder. Pharmacies must have a plan in place to manage these situations, which may involve finding alternative suppliers, substituting medications where appropriate, or communicating with patients about the delay. For instance, if a particular brand of medication is unavailable, the pharmacist might offer a generic equivalent or suggest a different treatment option in consultation with the prescribing physician.

2.4.1 Pharmacy Licenses and Permits in India

In India, operating a community pharmacy requires adherence to a comprehensive set of legal requirements, including obtaining the necessary licenses and permits. These legal obligations are designed to ensure that pharmacies maintain high standards of practice, safeguard public health, and comply with national and state regulations. Understanding and fulfilling these requirements is crucial for anyone looking to establish or manage a pharmacy in India.

Pharmacy licenses are issued by the respective State Drug Control Organization, and obtaining them is a mandatory step before a pharmacy can commence operations. The primary license required is the Retail Drug License (RDL), which authorizes the sale of medicines to the general public. This license is regulated under the Drugs and Cosmetics Act, 1940, and the Drugs and Cosmetics Rules, 1945.

To obtain an RDL, the applicant must meet specific criteria, including employing a registered pharmacist in the pharmacy. The pharmacist must possess valid registration with the State Pharmacy Council and must be present in the pharmacy during operating hours to ensure compliance with regulatory requirements. The RDL is typically valid for five years, after which it needs to be renewed to continue the lawful operation of the pharmacy.

Another essential permit is the **Wholesale Drug License** (WDL), which is required if the pharmacy intends to engage in the wholesale distribution of medicines. Similar to the RDL, the WDL is governed by the Drugs and Cosmetics Act and Rules. The applicant must provide proof of ownership or lease agreement for the premises, details of storage facilities, and information about the qualified person in charge of the wholesale operations. The WDL ensures that the pharmacy complies with the necessary storage and handling requirements for large quantities of medicines.

In addition to these licenses, pharmacies dealing with **narcotics and psychotropic substances** must obtain a special permit under the Narcotic Drugs and Psychotropic Substances (NDPS) Act, 1985. This permit is issued by the Narcotics Control Bureau and is required for the sale, purchase, or distribution of controlled substances. The pharmacy must adhere to strict guidelines regarding the storage, dispensing, and record-keeping of these substances to prevent misuse and illegal distribution. Failure to comply with the NDPS Act can result in severe penalties, including revocation of the pharmacy's licenses and legal action against the pharmacy owner.

Pharmacies must also obtain a **Good Distribution Practice (GDP) certification** if they wish to participate in the export of pharmaceuticals. The GDP certification ensures that the pharmacy adheres to internationally recognized standards for the storage, transportation, and distribution of medicines. This certification is particularly important for pharmacies that supply medicines to international markets, as it validates their commitment to quality and safety in the supply chain.

The **registration of the pharmacy premises** is another crucial legal requirement. The premises must be registered with the local municipal authorities, and the pharmacy must comply with local zoning laws and regulations. The premises should meet the standards set by the Drugs and Cosmetics Act, including adequate space, proper storage facilities, and suitable environmental conditions for storing medicines. Regular inspections by drug inspectors are conducted to ensure that the pharmacy adheres to these standards, and any violations can lead to penalties or suspension of licenses.

In addition to the above, pharmacies must maintain **appropriate records and documentation** as part of their legal obligations. This includes maintaining registers for the sale of prescription drugs, records of controlled substances, and invoices for all purchases and sales. The records must be accurate and up-to-date, as they may be reviewed by regulatory authorities during inspections. Proper documentation not only ensures compliance with legal requirements but also helps in maintaining transparency and accountability in pharmacy operations.

Lastly, it is essential for pharmacy owners and staff to stay informed about any changes in the legal framework governing pharmacies in India. The regulatory landscape is dynamic, with new rules and amendments being introduced regularly. For instance, recent developments in the regulation of online pharmacies and e-pharmacies have introduced additional licensing and compliance requirements for digital platforms that sell medicines. Keeping abreast of these changes and ensuring that the pharmacy complies with all relevant laws is vital for avoiding

2.4.2 Compliance with Drug Regulations

Compliance with drug regulations is a critical aspect of operating a community pharmacy in India. The regulatory framework governing the sale, distribution, and dispensing of drugs is designed to ensure the safety, efficacy, and quality of medicines available to the public. It is the responsibility of the pharmacy owner and staff to adhere to these regulations to maintain the integrity of the pharmacy's operations and protect public health.

The primary legislation governing drug regulation in India is the **Drugs and Cosmetics Act, 1940**, along with the **Drugs and Cosmetics Rules, 1945**. These laws provide the legal framework for the control and regulation of the import, manufacture, distribution, and sale of drugs and cosmetics in India. Compliance with these laws is mandatory for all pharmacies, and failure to adhere to them can result in severe penalties, including fines, imprisonment, and revocation of licenses.

One of the key aspects of compliance is ensuring that the pharmacy only dispenses drugs that are approved by the **Central Drugs Standard Control Organization (CDSCO)** and are listed in the Indian Pharmacopoeia. Pharmacies must not stock or sell any drugs that are banned or unapproved by the CDSCO. Regular updates from the CDSCO must be monitored to stay informed about any changes in the status of medications, such as new approvals, recalls, or bans. For example, if a particular drug is found to have adverse effects and is subsequently banned, the pharmacy must immediately remove it from its shelves and stop its sale.

Prescription regulations are another critical component of compliance. According to the Drugs and Cosmetics Rules, certain categories of drugs, such as Schedule H and Schedule X drugs, can only be dispensed with a valid prescription from a registered medical practitioner. Pharmacies must strictly adhere to this rule and ensure that these medications are not sold over-the-counter. Proper records of all prescriptions must be maintained, including the name of the prescribing doctor, the name and address of the patient, and the details of the medication dispensed. These records are subject to inspection by drug control authorities, and any discrepancies can lead to legal action.

Pharmacies must also comply with the **storage requirements** stipulated by the Drugs and Cosmetics Rules. This includes maintaining appropriate temperature and humidity levels for different types of medications, particularly those that are temperature-sensitive, such as vaccines and insulin. The pharmacy must have adequate facilities, such as refrigeration units, to store these medications properly. Regular monitoring of storage conditions is essential to ensure that the medications retain their efficacy and are safe for consumption.

Another important aspect of compliance is the **labeling and packaging** of drugs. The Drugs and Cosmetics Rules prescribe specific requirements for the labeling of medications, including the name of the drug, dosage form, strength, batch number, manufacturing date, expiry date, and the name and address of the manufacturer. Labels must also include any special storage instructions, such as "Keep out of reach of children" or "Store in a cool, dry place." Compliance with these labeling requirements is essential to ensure that patients receive accurate information about their medications and to prevent medication errors.

Pharmacies must also comply with the regulations concerning the **disposal of expired or damaged drugs**. The Drugs and Cosmetics Rules mandate that expired or damaged drugs should not be sold or dispensed to patients. Such drugs must be segregated from the regular stock and disposed of in accordance with the guidelines provided by the CDSCO and local environmental regulations. Proper documentation of the disposal process is required to ensure transparency and accountability.

Adverse drug reaction (ADR) reporting is another crucial aspect of compliance. Pharmacies are encouraged to participate in the Pharmacovigilance Program of India (PvPI) by reporting any adverse drug reactions observed in patients. This contributes to the monitoring of drug safety and helps in identifying potential risks associated with medications. Pharmacists should be trained to recognize ADRs and understand the process of reporting them to the relevant authorities.

2.5.1 Prescription Register

The maintenance of a prescription register is a critical aspect of pharmacy management, serving as a vital record-keeping tool that ensures compliance with legal requirements, facilitates auditing, and promotes patient safety. A well-maintained prescription register provides a comprehensive and accurate record of all prescriptions dispensed by the pharmacy, helping to protect both the pharmacy and its patients.

The **primary purpose** of a prescription register is to document the details of every prescription that is filled. This includes recording the name of the patient, the name and dosage of the medication, the quantity dispensed, the prescribing doctor's name, and the date of dispensing. These details are crucial for ensuring that the pharmacy has a clear and traceable record of all medications dispensed, which is essential in case of any queries or disputes regarding a prescription. For example, if a patient questions whether they received the correct medication or dosage, the pharmacy can refer to the prescription register to verify the details of the transaction.

In India, maintaining a prescription register is particularly important for medications that fall under **Schedule H and Schedule X** of the Drugs and Cosmetics Rules, 1945. These schedules include drugs that require a prescription due to their potential for misuse or adverse effects. The register must be meticulously maintained to ensure that all transactions involving these drugs are accurately recorded and that the pharmacy is in compliance with the legal requirements. Failure to maintain a proper prescription register can result in legal penalties, including fines or suspension of the pharmacy's license.

Accuracy and completeness are paramount in maintaining a prescription register. Every entry must be made in a timely manner, ensuring that no prescriptions are left unrecorded. The information recorded must be complete, without any omissions, as incomplete records can lead to difficulties in tracking and auditing. Pharmacies should establish clear procedures for entering information into the register, and staff should be trained to follow these procedures diligently. For instance, when a prescription is filled, the pharmacist or pharmacy technician should immediately record the transaction in the register before handing the medication to the patient.

The **format and organization** of the prescription register should be standardized to facilitate easy access and retrieval of information. Most pharmacies maintain their registers in a chronological order, with entries made on the day the prescription is filled. Each entry is typically assigned a unique identification number, which can be used to quickly locate specific prescriptions. In addition to the physical register, many modern pharmacies use computerized systems to maintain electronic prescription registers. These systems offer the advantage of quick searches, automatic updates, and integration with other pharmacy management tools, such as inventory management systems. However, even with electronic registers, it is important to regularly back up the data to prevent loss in case of system failures.

Regulatory authorities may conduct inspections to ensure that the prescription register is being properly maintained. During such inspections, the authorities may review the register to verify that all prescriptions, particularly those for controlled substances, have been accurately recorded. They may also check for any discrepancies between the register and the physical stock of medications. Pharmacies must be prepared for these inspections by ensuring that their prescription register is up-to-date, accurate, and readily accessible.

The prescription register also plays a key role in **auditing and accountability**. It allows the pharmacy to track the dispensing patterns of medications, identify any unusual or potentially problematic transactions, and ensure that all prescriptions have been filled according to the legal and ethical standards. For example, if a particular medication is being prescribed at an unusually high frequency, the pharmacy can investigate to ensure that there is no inappropriate prescribing or misuse. The register can also be used to verify that all prescriptions have been filled according to the doctor's orders, without any unauthorized substitutions or alterations.

2.5.2 Controlled Drugs Register

The Controlled Drugs Register is a crucial record that every community pharmacy must maintain to comply with legal requirements governing the handling of controlled substances. These substances, which include certain medications with a high potential for abuse or dependence, are strictly regulated under the Narcotic Drugs and Psychotropic Substances (NDPS) Act, 1985, in India. The Controlled Drugs Register is a vital tool for ensuring that these substances are managed responsibly and that the pharmacy adheres to all regulatory standards.

The **primary function** of the Controlled Drugs Register is to meticulously document all transactions involving controlled substances. This includes the receipt, storage, and dispensing of these drugs. For each transaction, the register must record detailed information such as the date of the transaction, the name and address of the supplier or customer, the quantity of the drug received or dispensed, the balance of the drug in stock, and the signature of the pharmacist responsible for the transaction. These records provide a comprehensive audit trail that helps in monitoring the movement of controlled substances within the pharmacy and ensuring that none are lost or diverted for illegal use.

Maintaining a **detailed and accurate register** is not just a regulatory requirement but also a critical aspect of ensuring patient safety. By keeping precise records, pharmacies can track the usage of controlled drugs and identify any irregularities that may indicate potential misuse or abuse. For example, if the register shows that a particular controlled drug is being dispensed more frequently than expected, this may prompt an investigation to determine whether the medication is being prescribed and used appropriately.

The Controlled Drugs Register must be **maintained separately** from other pharmacy records, and it should be kept in a secure location, accessible only to authorized personnel. This is to ensure that the information within the register is protected and that the integrity of the records is maintained. The register itself must be in a bound book or an electronic format that is tamper-evident, meaning that entries cannot be easily altered or deleted. Each page of the register must be numbered sequentially to prevent the removal or addition of pages. In the case of electronic registers, adequate security measures, such as access controls and audit logs, must be in place to prevent unauthorized access or tampering.

Regular auditing of the Controlled Drugs Register is essential to ensure that the records are accurate and up-to-date. This involves reconciling the quantities of controlled drugs recorded in the register with the actual physical stock in the pharmacy. Any discrepancies between the two must be investigated immediately, and appropriate corrective actions must be taken. Regular audits help in identifying potential issues early and ensuring that the pharmacy remains in compliance with legal requirements. In addition to internal audits, regulatory authorities may conduct inspections to review the Controlled Drugs Register and verify that all records are in order. Pharmacies must be prepared for these inspections by maintaining their registers in strict accordance with the law.

Documentation of destroyed or returned controlled drugs is another important aspect of the Controlled Drugs Register. If a controlled drug is expired, damaged, or otherwise no longer needed, it must be destroyed in accordance with regulatory guidelines. The destruction of controlled drugs must be witnessed by a qualified professional, and the details of the destruction, including the date, method, and witnesses, must be recorded in the register. Similarly, if a controlled drug is returned to the supplier, this transaction must be fully documented in the register, with all relevant details recorded. These procedures ensure that controlled drugs are not misused or diverted after they have been deemed unfit for patient use.

2.6.1 Business Software

The integration of business software in community pharmacies has revolutionized the way these establishments operate, enhancing efficiency, accuracy, and overall service quality. Business software in a pharmacy setting typically includes a range of applications designed to manage various aspects of the business, such as inventory control, billing, patient records, and regulatory compliance. The use of these systems allows pharmacists to streamline operations, reduce manual errors, and focus more on patient care rather than administrative tasks.

One of the most critical functions of business software in a pharmacy is **inventory management**. Inventory control is a complex task that involves tracking thousands of medications, each with different expiration dates, storage requirements, and reorder levels. Business software automates this process by keeping real-time records of stock levels, automatically alerting staff when a particular drug is running low, and generating purchase orders as needed. For example, the software can track the usage patterns of common medications, predict when stocks will deplete, and ensure that the pharmacy is always well-stocked without overstocking, which can lead to waste. Additionally, the software can monitor the shelf life of medications, ensuring that those nearing expiration are used first or flagged for return to the supplier.

Billing and financial management are also significantly improved through the use of business software. Pharmacy management systems can handle various forms of payment, including cash, credit cards, and insurance claims, ensuring that all transactions are recorded accurately. The software can process insurance claims electronically, reducing the time and effort required to submit claims manually. This not only speeds up the payment process but also minimizes the chances of errors that could lead to claim rejections. Furthermore, the software generates detailed financial reports, helping the pharmacy to track its income, expenses, and profitability. These reports are invaluable for making informed business decisions, such as adjusting pricing strategies or identifying areas where cost savings can be achieved.

Another essential feature of business software in community pharmacies is the **management of patient records**. Modern pharmacy systems include electronic health records (EHR) that store comprehensive patient information, including medication history, allergies, and previous interactions with the pharmacy. This information is easily accessible to pharmacists when dispensing medications, allowing them to verify prescriptions, check for potential drug interactions, and provide personalized advice to patients. For instance, if a patient has a known allergy to a particular drug, the system can automatically alert the pharmacist if a prescription for that drug is entered, preventing potential harm. Additionally, patient records can be used to monitor adherence to prescribed therapies, enabling the pharmacist to follow up with patients who may be at risk of non-compliance.

Regulatory compliance is another critical area where business software plays a vital role. Pharmacies are subject to numerous regulations regarding the handling, dispensing, and record-keeping of medications, especially controlled substances. Business software helps pharmacies maintain compliance by ensuring that all transactions are recorded accurately and that all necessary documentation is generated and stored securely. The software can also automate the generation of reports required by regulatory bodies, such as the Drugs Controller General of India (DCGI) or the Narcotics Control Bureau. This reduces the administrative burden on pharmacy staff and ensures that the pharmacy remains compliant with all legal requirements, thus avoiding penalties or legal issues.

Customer relationship management (CRM) is also enhanced through the use of business software. Many pharmacy management systems include CRM features that help pharmacists build stronger relationships with their customers. These features may include automated reminders for prescription refills, personalized health tips based on the customer's medication history, and loyalty programs that reward frequent customers. By leveraging these tools, pharmacies can improve customer satisfaction and retention, which is crucial for long-term business success. For example, a pharmacy might use the CRM system to send a text message to a patient reminding them to refill their prescription or to offer a discount on their next purchase.

2.6.2 Healthcare Software

Healthcare software is an integral component of modern community pharmacy management, playing a critical role in enhancing patient care, ensuring medication safety, and improving overall operational efficiency. Unlike business software, which primarily focuses on the financial and logistical aspects of running a pharmacy, healthcare software is specifically designed to manage clinical information, support clinical decisions, and streamline the delivery of healthcare services.

One of the primary functions of healthcare software in a pharmacy setting is **electronic prescribing (e-prescribing)**. E-prescribing systems allow healthcare providers to send prescriptions directly to the pharmacy electronically, eliminating the need for handwritten prescriptions. This not only reduces the risk of errors caused by illegible handwriting but also speeds up the dispensing process. With e-prescribing, pharmacists can quickly receive and process prescriptions, verify insurance coverage, and prepare medications for pickup or delivery. Additionally, e-prescribing systems often include features that alert prescribers to potential drug interactions, allergies, or dosage errors before the prescription is finalized, thereby enhancing patient safety.

Clinical decision support systems (CDSS) are another vital aspect of healthcare software used in community pharmacies. CDSS tools are integrated into pharmacy management systems to assist pharmacists in making informed decisions about patient care. These systems analyze patient data, including their medication history, allergies, and current prescriptions, to provide evidence-based recommendations. For instance, if a patient is prescribed a new medication that could interact negatively with a drug they are already taking, the CDSS will alert the pharmacist to this potential interaction. The pharmacist can then consult with the prescribing physician to adjust the treatment plan if necessary. CDSS also helps in ensuring that prescribed dosages are appropriate for the patient's age, weight, and renal function, further minimizing the risk of adverse drug events.

Medication therapy management (MTM) software is another important tool used in community pharmacies. MTM software helps pharmacists conduct comprehensive medication reviews, develop personalized medication-related action plans, and monitor patients' progress over time. These systems are particularly beneficial for managing patients with chronic conditions who are on complex medication regimens. The software allows pharmacists to track patients' adherence to their prescribed therapies, identify any barriers to adherence, and provide tailored interventions to improve outcomes. For example, if the software indicates that a patient is consistently missing doses of a particular medication, the pharmacist can intervene by providing adherence tools, such as pill organizers or reminder apps, and counseling the patient on the importance of taking their medications as prescribed.

Patient health records (PHR) are also managed through healthcare software. PHR systems store detailed records of each patient's medical history, including their medications, laboratory results, and immunization records. These records are crucial for providing continuity of care, especially when patients are seen by multiple healthcare providers. By having access to a patient's comprehensive health record, pharmacists can make more informed decisions about their care, identify potential issues, and coordinate with other healthcare providers as needed. For instance, if a patient has recently been hospitalized, the pharmacist can review the discharge summary and adjust the patient's medication regimen accordingly to avoid duplications or contraindications.

Telepharmacy is an emerging area where healthcare software plays a significant role. Telepharmacy platforms enable pharmacists to provide remote consultations, medication reviews, and other healthcare services to patients who may not be able to visit the pharmacy in person. These platforms typically include video conferencing capabilities, secure messaging, and integration with electronic health records. Telepharmacy not only expands access to pharmacy services but also allows pharmacists to maintain regular contact with patients, monitor their treatment progress, and provide timely interventions when necessary. For example, a pharmacist can use telepharmacy software to conduct a follow-up consultation with a patient who has started a new medication, ensuring that they are taking it correctly and addressing any side effects they may be experiencing.

Immunization management software is another key component of healthcare software used in community pharmacies. This software helps pharmacists manage and track immunizations provided to patients, ensuring that all vaccinations are recorded accurately and that patients receive the appropriate follow-up doses. The software can also generate reminders for upcoming vaccinations, alerting both the pharmacist and the patient when a booster dose is due. This is particularly important for managing vaccines that require multiple doses over a specific time period, such as the COVID-19 vaccine or the HPV vaccine.

THREE

PRESCRIPTION HANDLING IN COMMUNITY PHARMACY

3.1.1 Patient Information

The patient information section is one of the most critical parts of a prescription, as it contains essential details about the individual for whom the medication is being prescribed. Accurate and complete patient information is vital for ensuring that the correct medication is dispensed to the right person and that the pharmacy can provide appropriate care and advice tailored to the patient's specific needs.

The **patient's name** is the first and most obvious piece of information in this section. It must be recorded accurately, including the correct spelling, as any errors can lead to confusion or even the dispensing of medication to the wrong person. In some cases, especially in pediatric prescriptions, it may also include the patient's age or date of birth to differentiate between patients with similar names. For example, if two patients named "Rahul Sharma" are being treated in the same facility, their ages or dates of birth would help the pharmacist ensure that the correct Rahul Sharma receives the prescribed medication.

Next, the **patient's address** is typically included on the prescription. This serves multiple purposes: it helps verify the patient's identity, particularly in cases where the medication is delivered or collected by someone other than the patient, and it allows the pharmacy to send any necessary follow-up information or reminders directly to the patient's home. The address also provides context regarding the patient's location, which can be important for public health monitoring and for ensuring that the patient has access to a pharmacy that can meet their ongoing needs.

The **contact information** of the patient, usually a phone number, is another important detail. This allows the pharmacy to reach out to the patient if there are any issues or questions regarding the prescription, such as clarifying dosages or discussing potential drug interactions. Contact information is also crucial for notifying the patient when their medication is ready for pickup or delivery. For instance, if a prescription requires a special order or takes longer to prepare, the pharmacy can quickly inform the patient of any delays or changes.

In addition to these basic details, the **patient's age and gender** are often recorded on the prescription. These details are important because they can influence the type of medication prescribed, the dosage, and the form in which the medication is administered. For example, certain medications may be contraindicated for specific age groups or require dosage adjustments based on age. Similarly, some medications may have different efficacy or side effects depending on the patient's gender, making this information essential for safe and effective treatment.

In some cases, the patient's **weight** may also be included, especially when prescribing medications where the dosage is weight-dependent. This is common in pediatric prescriptions or for certain drugs such as chemotherapy agents, anticoagulants, or anesthetics, where accurate dosing is critical for efficacy and safety. Recording the patient's weight on the prescription helps the pharmacist verify that the prescribed dose is appropriate, reducing the risk of underdosing or overdosing.

The **patient's medical history** and **allergies** are also crucial pieces of information that may be referenced when processing a prescription. While these details might not always be directly included on the prescription itself, they are often available in the pharmacy's patient records. Knowing a patient's medical history allows the pharmacist to check for potential drug interactions, contraindications, or previous adverse reactions to similar medications. For instance, if a patient has a documented allergy to penicillin, the pharmacist can identify this and contact the prescribing doctor to suggest an alternative antibiotic.

Finally, the **patient's identification number** or other identifiers, such as a hospital or clinic registration number, may be included on the prescription. This is particularly important in settings where multiple patients might share similar names, as it provides an additional layer of verification. These identifiers ensure that the prescription is correctly matched to the patient's electronic health record, facilitating the integration of the prescription into the broader healthcare management system.

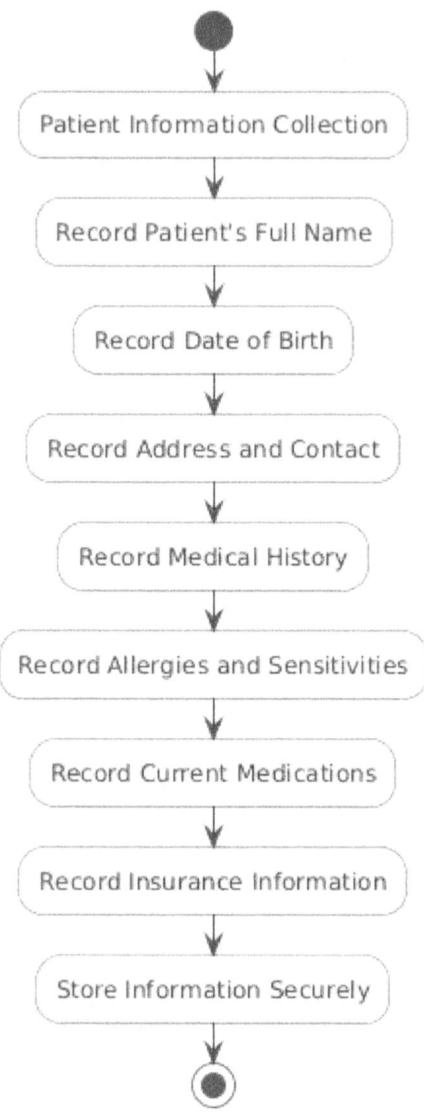

Flowchart for Patient Information Management

3.1.2 Medication Information

The medication information section of a prescription is at the heart of the document, as it provides the specific details necessary for dispensing the correct medication in the appropriate form and dosage. This section contains vital information that guides the pharmacist in ensuring that the patient receives the exact treatment prescribed by their healthcare provider. Accurate medication information is essential to prevent errors and ensure the efficacy and safety of the treatment.

The **name of the medication** is the first critical component in this section. It is essential that the medication name is clearly written and unambiguous to avoid any confusion or errors in dispensing. In many cases, both the generic name and the brand name of the medication are included to ensure clarity. For instance, a prescription might list "Paracetamol (Tylenol)" to specify the drug and its commonly known brand. Using the generic name is particularly important as it helps to prevent misunderstandings if the same drug is marketed under different brand names or if a generic equivalent is to be dispensed.

Dosage is the next key piece of information provided in this section. The dosage indicates the strength of the medication to be administered, typically expressed in milligrams (mg), micrograms (mcg), or other relevant units. For example, a prescription might specify "Amoxicillin 500 mg" to indicate the required dose of the medication. Accurate dosage information is crucial for ensuring that the patient receives the correct amount of medication, as an incorrect dosage can lead to ineffective treatment or harmful side effects. The dosage must be tailored to the patient's specific needs, taking into account factors such as age, weight, and the severity of the condition being treated.

Route of administration is another essential detail included in the medication information section. This indicates how the medication should be administered to the patient, whether orally, intravenously, topically, or by another method. For example, a prescription might state "Take 1 tablet orally" or "Apply ointment topically to the affected area." The route of administration is important because it influences how the drug is absorbed and metabolized by the body, and it ensures that the medication is delivered in the most effective manner for the patient's condition.

The **frequency and duration of treatment** are also specified in this section. The frequency indicates how often the medication should be taken, such as "twice daily" or "every 8 hours," while the duration specifies the length of time the treatment should continue, such as "for 7 days" or "until symptoms resolve." These instructions are critical for ensuring that the patient adheres to the treatment regimen and receives the full therapeutic benefit of the medication. For example, antibiotics are often prescribed with specific instructions to be taken for a full course of treatment, even if the patient feels better before the medication is finished, to prevent the development of antibiotic resistance.

Quantity to be dispensed is another important detail in the medication information section. This specifies the total amount of medication that the pharmacist should provide to the patient, often based on the dosage and duration of treatment. For instance, if a patient is prescribed "Take 1 tablet twice daily for 10 days," the quantity to be dispensed would be 20 tablets. Accurate calculation of the quantity is essential to ensure that the patient receives enough medication to complete their course of treatment without having to return to the pharmacy prematurely.

In some cases, the medication information section may also include **special instructions or warnings**. These are additional details provided by the prescriber to ensure the safe and effective use of the medication. For example, a prescription might include instructions such as "Take with food to avoid stomach upset" or "Do not drive or operate heavy machinery while taking this medication." These instructions help to inform the patient of any precautions they should take while using the medication and to avoid potential side effects or interactions with other substances.

The medication information section may also include the **refill information**, indicating whether the prescription can be refilled and, if so, how many times. This is particularly important for medications used in chronic conditions, where ongoing treatment is required. The prescriber may specify "Refill 3 times" or "No refills," depending on the treatment plan and the need for further evaluation before continuing the medication.

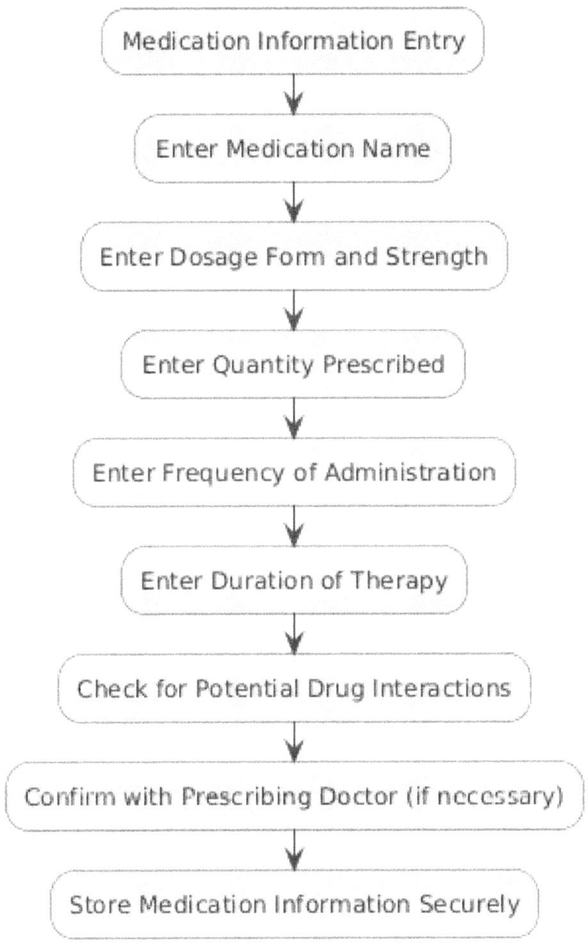

Medication information process

3.1.3 Directions for Use

The "Directions for Use" section of a prescription is crucial as it provides the patient with specific instructions on how to take or use the prescribed medication. This section guides the patient on the correct method and timing of administration, ensuring that the medication is used effectively and safely. Clear and precise directions help to prevent misunderstandings that could lead to improper use, decreased efficacy, or adverse effects.

The **dosage instructions** are a fundamental part of the directions for use. This includes not only the amount of medication to be taken at each dose but also how often it should be taken. For example, a prescription might instruct the patient to "Take one tablet every 8 hours," which clearly indicates that the medication should be taken three times a day, spaced evenly throughout the day. These instructions must be followed precisely to maintain the correct level of medication in the bloodstream and ensure its effectiveness. Inadequate or excessive dosing intervals can result in subtherapeutic levels or toxicity, respectively.

Timing of doses is another critical aspect covered in this section. Some medications must be taken at specific times of the day, with or without food, or at evenly spaced intervals. For instance, a prescription might specify "Take 30 minutes before meals" or "Take at bedtime." These instructions help optimize the absorption and action of the medication. For example, certain medications for acid reflux are more effective when taken before meals, while some antihypertensives work best when taken in the evening to control blood pressure during sleep.

Method of administration is also included in the directions for use. This tells the patient exactly how to take the medication, such as orally, via inhalation, topically, or through injection. For instance, the prescription might state "Take one capsule by mouth" or "Apply a thin layer of cream to the affected area twice daily." Clear instructions on the method of administration are essential to ensure that the medication is delivered to the correct site of action and in the appropriate manner. Misunderstanding these directions can lead to incorrect administration, reducing the drug's effectiveness or causing harm.

Special instructions may also be provided to guide the patient in the safe and effective use of the medication. These might include instructions to avoid certain foods, beverages, or activities while taking the medication. For example, a prescription might advise "Avoid grapefruit juice while taking this medication" or "Do not drive or operate heavy machinery after taking." Such instructions are included to prevent potential interactions that could alter the medication's effects or to minimize the risk of side effects. For example, grapefruit juice can interfere with the metabolism of certain drugs, leading to higher than intended levels in the bloodstream.

The directions for use may also include **advice on missed doses**. Patients are often advised on what to do if they forget to take a dose, such as "If you miss a dose, take it as soon as you remember, but skip the missed dose if it's almost time for your next dose." This guidance helps prevent double dosing, which can lead to overdose and serious side effects. Similarly, instructions might be given on how to handle vomiting after taking a dose, such as whether to retake the medication or wait until the next scheduled dose.

Duration of treatment is another important instruction that is often included. This tells the patient how long they should continue taking the medication. For example, a prescription might specify "Continue for 7 days" or "Take until all tablets are finished." It is crucial for patients to understand that even if they feel better before finishing the course, they should continue taking the medication as prescribed to ensure complete eradication of an infection or full therapeutic benefit. This is particularly important in the case of antibiotics, where incomplete courses can lead to the development of resistant strains of bacteria.

In some cases, the directions for use may also provide instructions on **storage** of the medication. This might include advice such as "Store in a cool, dry place" or "Refrigerate after opening." Proper storage ensures that the medication maintains its potency and safety until it is fully used. Failure to store medications correctly can result in degradation, rendering the medication less effective or even harmful.

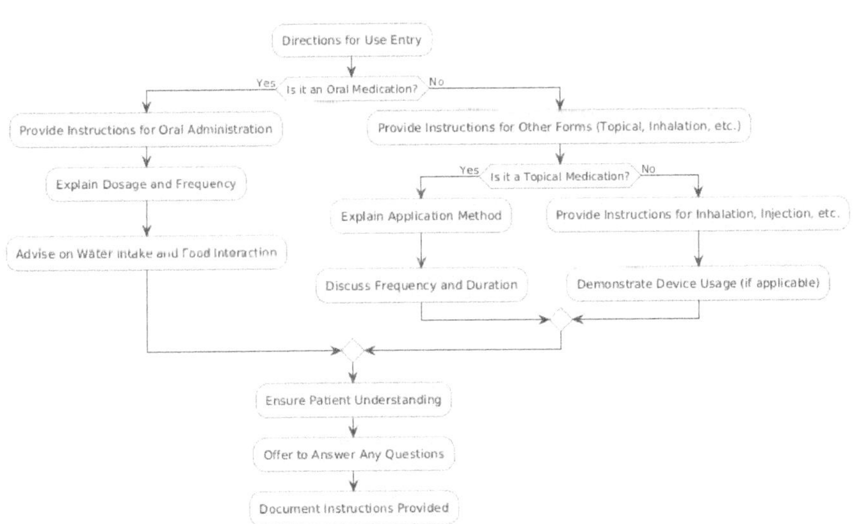

Guidelines for Providing Medication Use Instructions

3.2.1 Validity and Authentication of Prescriptions

The validity and authentication of prescriptions are fundamental aspects of legal compliance in community pharmacy practice. Ensuring that a prescription is valid and authentic is not only a legal requirement but also a critical step in safeguarding patient safety and preventing the misuse of medications. Pharmacists must carefully assess each prescription to verify that it meets all the necessary legal criteria before dispensing any medication.

A prescription is considered **valid** if it is issued by a registered and qualified medical practitioner who is authorized to prescribe medications. In India, this generally includes doctors, dentists, and certain other healthcare professionals who are registered with their respective councils. The pharmacist must verify the prescriber's qualifications, which are typically indicated by the professional titles (e.g., Dr., DDS) and registration numbers included on the prescription. For instance, a prescription from a general practitioner should include the doctor's name, registration number, and the details of the healthcare facility where they practice. This information ensures that the prescriber has the legal authority to prescribe the medications listed.

Authentication of the prescription involves verifying that the document is genuine and has not been tampered with. This process includes checking for the prescriber's signature, which must be present and match the signature on file, if available. In cases where the pharmacist is familiar with the prescriber, they can use their knowledge of the prescriber's signature and handwriting style to authenticate the prescription. For digital prescriptions, the pharmacist must ensure that the electronic signature or authentication code is valid and that the prescription was transmitted through a secure, recognized platform. For example, an e-prescription sent through a certified health information exchange should include a verifiable digital signature to confirm its authenticity.

The **date of issuance** is another critical factor in determining the validity of a prescription. In India, the validity of a prescription generally depends on the type of medication prescribed. For example, prescriptions for Schedule H drugs, which include antibiotics and other critical medications, are typically valid for one month from the date of issuance. Prescriptions for Schedule X drugs, which include controlled substances, may have more stringent validity periods and additional requirements for dispensing. The pharmacist must ensure that the prescription is filled within the valid time frame; otherwise, the patient may need to obtain a new prescription. Filling an expired prescription is not only illegal but also risky, as the patient's medical condition may have changed since the prescription was issued.

Controlled substances require additional scrutiny during the validation and authentication process. These substances, which include certain painkillers, sedatives, and stimulants, are subject to strict regulations due to their potential for abuse and dependence. The prescription for a controlled substance must include specific details such as the patient's full name and address, the prescriber's full details including their registration number, and the exact dosage and quantity of the medication. The pharmacist must also ensure that the prescription adheres to the regulatory requirements outlined in the Narcotic Drugs and Psychotropic Substances (NDPS) Act, 1985. For instance, a prescription for a Schedule X drug should not be refilled unless explicitly authorized by the prescriber, and the pharmacist must maintain accurate records of the dispensed medication.

In addition to verifying the prescriber's authority and the prescription's authenticity, the pharmacist must also assess the **completeness** of the prescription. A valid prescription should include all necessary details, such as the patient's name, age, and address, the name and dosage of the medication, the quantity to be dispensed, and clear instructions for use. If any of this information is missing or unclear, the pharmacist should contact the prescriber for clarification before dispensing the medication. For example, if a prescription lacks dosage instructions, the pharmacist must verify the correct dosage with the prescriber to prevent potential dosing errors.

Pharmacy laws and regulations also require pharmacists to maintain accurate records of all prescriptions filled, particularly those for controlled substances. These records must be readily available for inspection by regulatory authorities and should include details such as the date of dispensing, the quantity of medication provided, and the name of the pharmacist who dispensed the prescription. Maintaining these records not only ensures compliance with legal requirements but also provides a traceable history of medication dispensed, which can be vital in cases of drug recalls or investigations into prescription fraud.

3.2.2 Record-Keeping Requirements

Record-keeping is a fundamental aspect of prescription handling in community pharmacies, serving both legal and operational purposes. Proper documentation ensures that pharmacies comply with regulatory requirements, maintain accountability, and provide a traceable history of all medications dispensed. Accurate record-keeping is essential for safeguarding patient safety, preventing medication errors, and enabling effective auditing and oversight by regulatory authorities.

In India, the **Drugs and Cosmetics Act, 1940**, along with the **Drugs and Cosmetics Rules, 1945**, mandates that pharmacies maintain comprehensive records of all prescriptions filled. These records must include specific details such as the patient's name, the name and dosage of the medication, the prescribing doctor's name, the date of dispensing, and the quantity of medication provided. For example, when dispensing a prescription for an antibiotic like amoxicillin, the pharmacist must record the patient's information, the exact dosage prescribed, and the number of tablets or capsules dispensed. This ensures that there is a clear and traceable record of the medication's movement from the pharmacy to the patient.

One of the most critical aspects of record-keeping is the **maintenance of prescription records** for controlled substances. Controlled substances, such as certain painkillers, sedatives, and stimulants, are subject to stringent regulations due to their potential for abuse and addiction. The **Narcotic Drugs and Psychotropic Substances (NDPS) Act, 1985** requires that pharmacies keep detailed records of all transactions involving controlled substances. These records must include the full name and address of the patient, the name and address of the prescriber, the exact dosage and quantity of the drug dispensed, and the date of the transaction. Additionally, pharmacies must maintain separate registers for different categories of controlled substances, such as Schedule H and Schedule X drugs, to ensure that these records are easily accessible for inspection by regulatory authorities.

Retention periods for prescription records are also an important consideration in record-keeping requirements. According to Indian regulations, pharmacies must retain prescription records for a minimum of two years from the date of the last entry. However, for controlled substances, the retention period may be longer, depending on the specific requirements of the NDPS Act and other relevant laws. For example, records of Schedule X drugs must be kept for a minimum of five years. These retention periods ensure that records are available for review during inspections or audits and that they can be used as evidence in legal or regulatory proceedings if necessary.

In addition to paper records, many modern pharmacies use **electronic record-keeping systems** to manage prescription information. Electronic systems offer several advantages, including easier storage, faster retrieval of information, and improved accuracy. These systems can automatically update records when a prescription is filled, generate reports for regulatory compliance, and provide alerts for potential issues, such as duplicate prescriptions or drug interactions. For instance, an electronic system can flag a patient who has been prescribed two medications that could interact negatively, allowing the pharmacist to take corrective action before dispensing the drugs.

Confidentiality and security are paramount in the maintenance of prescription records. Pharmacies must ensure that all records, whether paper or electronic, are stored securely to protect patient privacy. Unauthorized access to these records can lead to breaches of patient confidentiality and potential legal consequences for the pharmacy. Physical records should be stored in locked cabinets or secure rooms, while electronic records should be protected by strong passwords, encryption, and access controls. For example, only authorized pharmacy staff should have access to prescription records, and electronic systems should log all access attempts to detect any unauthorized activity.

Regular audits of prescription records are necessary to ensure compliance with legal requirements and to identify any discrepancies or irregularities. Pharmacies should conduct internal audits periodically to review their record-keeping practices, verify the accuracy of their records, and ensure that all transactions are properly documented. Audits can also help to identify potential areas for improvement in the pharmacy's processes, such as the need for additional staff training on record-keeping procedures or the implementation of new technologies to enhance accuracy and efficiency.

3.3.1 Drug Interactions

Drug interactions are a significant concern in the management of patient medications within a community pharmacy. These interactions occur when the effects of one drug are altered by the presence of another drug, food, or even a medical condition, leading to either reduced efficacy or increased risk of adverse effects. Identifying and managing drug interactions is a critical responsibility of pharmacists, as these interactions can have serious implications for patient safety and treatment outcomes.

Types of Drug Interactions

Drug interactions can be broadly classified into three main types: **pharmacokinetic**, **pharmacodynamic**, and **pharmaceutical** interactions.

1. **Pharmacokinetic interactions** involve changes in the absorption, distribution, metabolism, or excretion of a drug, often resulting in altered drug levels in the bloodstream. For instance, certain drugs can inhibit or induce liver enzymes that metabolize other medications, leading to either increased toxicity or reduced therapeutic effect. A common example is the interaction between warfarin, an anticoagulant, and certain antibiotics like rifampin, which can induce the metabolism of warfarin, reducing its efficacy and increasing the risk of clot formation.
2. **Pharmacodynamic interactions** occur when two drugs affect the same physiological pathway or receptor, leading to additive, synergistic, or antagonistic effects. For example, taking two central nervous system depressants, such as benzodiazepines and opioids, can result in enhanced sedation and respiratory depression, increasing the risk of overdose. Pharmacodynamic interactions are particularly important when multiple drugs with similar effects are prescribed, as they can lead to an exaggerated response or increased risk of side effects.

Pharmaceutical interactions refer to incompatibilities that occur before the drug is even administered, such as when two drugs are mixed together in a syringe or IV solution and form a precipitate, reducing their effectiveness or safety. While less common in a community pharmacy setting, pharmacists must still be aware of potential pharmaceutical interactions, especially when preparing compounded medications or advising on the administration of injectable drugs.

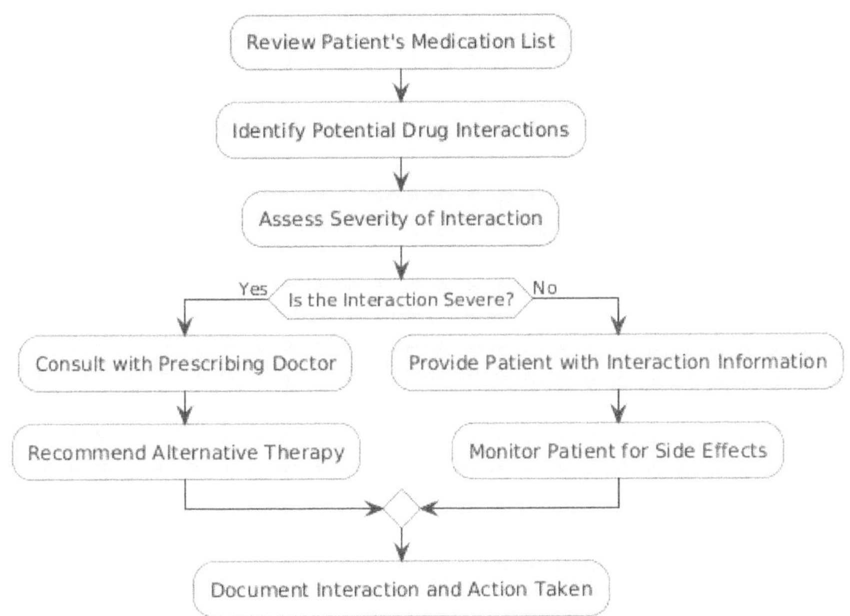

Process for Identifying and Managing Drug Interactions

Identification and Prevention

Pharmacists play a crucial role in identifying potential drug interactions before they can cause harm to the patient. This process typically involves reviewing the patient's complete medication profile, including all prescription and over-the-counter drugs, supplements, and herbal products. By assessing the potential for interactions between these substances, pharmacists can take proactive steps to prevent adverse effects.

Electronic health records (EHRs) and **drug interaction databases** are invaluable tools in this process. These systems can automatically flag potential interactions based on the patient's current medications, alerting the pharmacist to review the combination and take appropriate action. For example, if a patient is prescribed a new medication that could interact with an existing drug in their regimen, the software may alert the pharmacist to contact the prescriber for an alternative therapy or adjust the dosage to minimize the risk.

Patient education is another key aspect of managing drug interactions. Pharmacists must inform patients about the potential risks associated with their medications and advise them on how to avoid interactions. This might include instructions to take certain medications at different times of the day, avoid specific foods or beverages, or watch for signs of adverse effects. For instance, patients on statins may be advised to avoid grapefruit juice, as it can inhibit the metabolism of the drug, leading to higher blood levels and an increased risk of muscle toxicity.

Case Studies and Real-World Examples

Several real-world examples highlight the importance of vigilance in identifying and managing drug interactions. For example, the combination of ACE inhibitors, which are used to manage hypertension, and potassium-sparing diuretics can lead to hyperkalemia, a dangerous increase in blood potassium levels. Another example is the interaction between digoxin, a cardiac glycoside, and amiodarone, an antiarrhythmic agent, where amiodarone can increase digoxin levels, potentially leading to digoxin toxicity.

Role of Technology in Drug Interaction Management

With the increasing complexity of drug regimens, especially in elderly patients who may be on multiple medications, the use of technology has become essential in managing drug interactions. Advanced clinical decision support systems (CDSS) integrated into pharmacy management software can provide real-time alerts and recommendations, helping pharmacists to quickly identify and address potential interactions. These systems are particularly valuable in busy community pharmacy settings, where pharmacists must process numerous prescriptions each day and ensure that every patient receives safe and effective therapy.

3.3.2 Adverse Drug Reactions

Adverse drug reactions (ADRs) are a significant concern in the management of medications within a community pharmacy setting. An ADR is defined as any unintended, harmful reaction to a drug administered at normal doses for therapeutic purposes. These reactions can range from mild side effects to severe, life-threatening conditions, making it essential for pharmacists to be vigilant in identifying, managing, and preventing ADRs to ensure patient safety and effective therapy.

Types of Adverse Drug Reactions

ADRs are generally classified into two broad categories: **Type A (Augmented) reactions** and **Type B (Bizarre) reactions**.

1. **Type A reactions** are dose-dependent and predictable, often related to the pharmacological action of the drug. These reactions are the most common and include effects such as nausea from opioids or hypoglycemia from insulin. Type A reactions can often be managed by adjusting the dose or by providing supportive care to mitigate the side effects. For example, a patient experiencing mild gastrointestinal upset from nonsteroidal anti-inflammatory drugs (NSAIDs) might be advised to take the medication with food or switch to a less irritating alternative.
2. **Type B reactions** are not dose-dependent and are unpredictable, often involving immune-mediated responses or idiosyncratic reactions. These reactions can be severe and include conditions like anaphylaxis from penicillin or Stevens-Johnson syndrome from certain anticonvulsants. Type B reactions are more challenging to predict and manage because they do not correlate with the drug's known pharmacological properties. In such cases, the medication is typically discontinued immediately, and the patient may require urgent medical intervention.

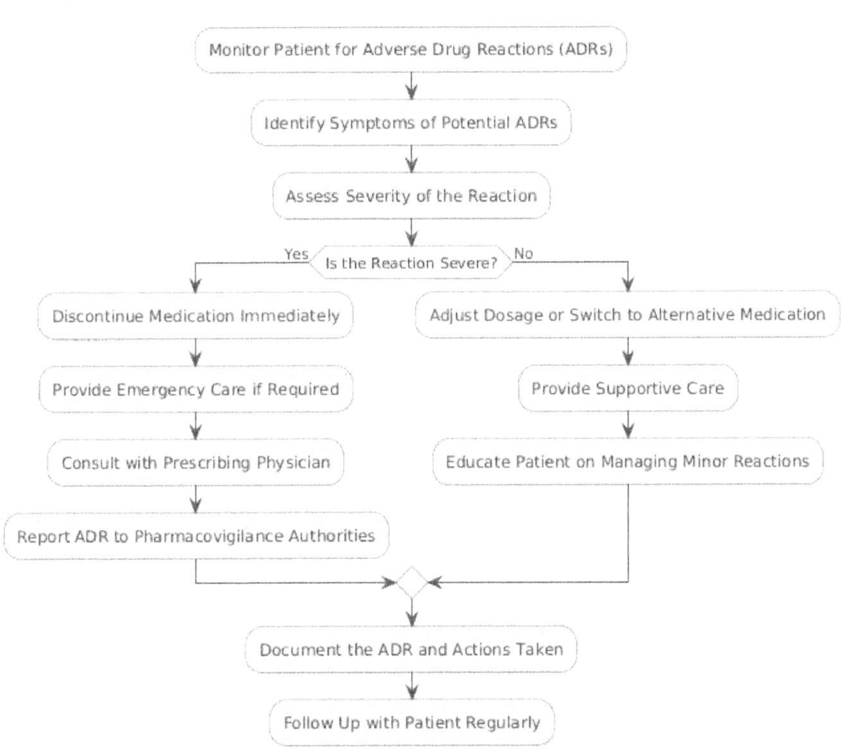

Adverse Drug Reactions Monitoring and Management Flowchart

Identification and Reporting

Pharmacists are often the first healthcare professionals to recognize an ADR, as they are directly involved in dispensing medications and monitoring patients' responses. Identifying an ADR requires a thorough understanding of the patient's medication history, as well as knowledge of the potential side effects associated with each drug. Pharmacists must be alert to any new symptoms reported by the patient, especially when they coincide with the initiation of a new medication.

In cases where an ADR is suspected, pharmacists must take appropriate action. This may involve advising the patient to stop taking the medication immediately, depending on the severity of the reaction, and referring them to their healthcare provider for further evaluation and treatment. In less severe cases, the pharmacist might recommend an alternative therapy or provide supportive measures to alleviate the symptoms.

Documentation and reporting of ADRs are crucial steps in managing these reactions. In India, pharmacists are encouraged to report ADRs to the Pharmacovigilance Program of India (PvPI), which is responsible for monitoring the safety of medicines and identifying new risks associated with their use. The reporting process involves filling out a detailed form that includes information about the patient, the suspected drug, the nature of the reaction, and the outcome. This data is collected and analyzed to detect patterns and trends that may indicate emerging safety concerns with specific medications.

Prevention and Risk Management

Preventing ADRs is a key responsibility of pharmacists and involves several strategies. One of the most effective methods is **medication reconciliation**, where the pharmacist reviews all of the patient's current medications, including prescription drugs, over-the-counter products, and supplements, to identify any potential risks. This process helps to prevent interactions and contraindications that could lead to ADRs. For example, a pharmacist might identify that a patient taking warfarin is also using a new herbal supplement known to increase the risk of bleeding and advise against its use.

Another important preventive measure is **patient education**. Pharmacists should provide clear instructions on how to take medications correctly, including dosage, timing, and any specific precautions, such as avoiding certain foods or activities. Educating patients about the potential side effects of their medications and advising them on what to do if they experience any adverse symptoms is crucial for early detection and management of ADRs. For instance, a patient starting on a new antihypertensive medication should be informed about the possibility of dizziness or lightheadedness and advised to get up slowly from a sitting or lying position to prevent falls.

Risk factors for ADRs, such as age, comorbidities, and polypharmacy, should also be considered when dispensing medications. Elderly patients, in particular, are more susceptible to ADRs due to age-related changes in drug metabolism and excretion, as well as the higher likelihood of multiple chronic conditions requiring complex drug regimens. In these cases, pharmacists should be especially cautious and may need to collaborate with the prescribing physician to adjust dosages or choose safer alternatives.

Case Studies and Examples

Real-world examples of ADRs underscore the importance of proactive management by pharmacists. For instance, a patient taking a statin may develop muscle pain and weakness, which could indicate statin-induced myopathy, a known ADR associated with this class of drugs. Early recognition and intervention by the pharmacist, such as recommending discontinuation of the statin and referring the patient for further evaluation, can prevent more serious complications.

Another example is the potential for ADRs in patients taking multiple medications that affect the central nervous system, such as benzodiazepines, opioids, and antidepressants. The pharmacist must be vigilant in monitoring these patients for signs of excessive sedation, respiratory depression, or other CNS-related side effects, which can be life-threatening if not promptly addressed.

3.3.3 Medication Errors

Medication errors are a significant concern in the healthcare system, particularly in the context of community pharmacies, where the safe and accurate dispensing of medications is paramount. A medication error is any preventable event that may cause or lead to inappropriate medication use or patient harm. These errors can occur at any stage of the medication-use process, from prescribing and transcribing to dispensing and administration. Understanding the types, causes, and prevention strategies for medication errors is essential for pharmacists to minimize their occurrence and ensure patient safety.

Types of Medication Errors

Medication errors can be broadly categorized into several types, each with distinct implications for patient safety:

1. **Prescribing Errors**: These occur when a healthcare provider writes a prescription that is incorrect or inappropriate. Common examples include prescribing the wrong drug, incorrect dosage, or inappropriate drug for the patient's condition. For instance, prescribing a medication without considering a patient's known allergy can result in a serious adverse reaction.
2. **Dispensing Errors**: These errors occur within the pharmacy when the wrong medication, dosage, or form is dispensed to the patient. This can happen due to mistakes such as selecting the wrong drug from the shelf, misreading the prescription, or incorrect labeling. For example, dispensing a 10 mg tablet instead of a 100 mg tablet can lead to underdosing and ineffective treatment.
3. **Administration Errors**: These occur when there is a mistake in giving the medication to the patient, either by the patient themselves or by healthcare personnel. Errors in administration include giving the wrong dose, administering the drug via the wrong route (e.g., oral vs. intravenous), or at the wrong time. For example, a patient instructed to take medication on an empty stomach but who takes it with food may not experience the full therapeutic effect.
4. **Monitoring Errors**: These happen when there is a failure to monitor the patient's response to the medication appropriately. This can include not checking for drug interactions, not monitoring blood levels of certain medications, or failing to follow up on potential side effects. For instance, not monitoring a diabetic patient's blood glucose levels while on a new hypoglycemic medication could lead to dangerous hypoglycemia.
5. **Documentation Errors**: These occur when there is a failure to accurately document the details of medication dispensing, administration, or monitoring. Incomplete or inaccurate records can lead to repeated errors and difficulties in tracking medication history.

Causes of Medication Errors

Several factors contribute to the occurrence of medication errors, and understanding these factors is crucial in developing strategies to prevent them:

1. **Human Factors**: These include errors due to fatigue, distractions, or lack of knowledge. For example, a pharmacist working long hours without adequate breaks may become fatigued and more prone to making dispensing errors. Similarly, distractions in a busy pharmacy environment can lead to mistakes in reading or interpreting prescriptions.
2. **Communication Failures**: Poor communication between healthcare providers, or between the pharmacist and the patient, can lead to errors. Miscommunication might involve unclear or incomplete instructions, misunderstandings, or failure to convey important information about the patient's health or medications. For instance, if a prescriber's handwriting is difficult to read, the pharmacist might misinterpret the prescription.
3. **System Failures**: These include issues related to the design and functioning of healthcare systems, such as inadequate electronic prescribing systems, poorly designed medication labels, or lack of standard protocols. For example, if a pharmacy's computer system does not adequately flag potential drug interactions, harmful combinations of medications may be dispensed.
4. **Patient-Related Factors**: Patients themselves can contribute to medication errors through non-adherence, misunderstandings about how to take their medications, or by not communicating all relevant health information to their healthcare providers. For instance, a patient who does not disclose that they are taking over-the-counter supplements may inadvertently cause a harmful interaction with a prescribed drug.

Prevention of Medication Errors

Preventing medication errors requires a multifaceted approach that involves pharmacists, healthcare providers, and patients working together to ensure safe medication practices:

1. **Education and Training**: Continuous education and training for pharmacists and pharmacy staff on the latest medication guidelines, error prevention strategies, and the use of technology are critical. This can include training on proper prescription interpretation, error reporting systems, and the use of clinical decision support tools.

2. **Use of Technology**: Implementing advanced technology systems, such as electronic prescribing (e-prescribing), barcode scanning for medication verification, and clinical decision support systems (CDSS), can significantly reduce the risk of errors. For example, e-prescribing systems can reduce errors related to illegible handwriting, while barcode scanning ensures that the correct medication is selected and dispensed.
3. **Standardization of Procedures**: Developing and adhering to standardized procedures for dispensing, labeling, and patient counseling can help minimize errors. For example, implementing a double-check system where two pharmacists verify the prescription before it is dispensed can catch potential errors before they reach the patient.
4. **Effective Communication**: Enhancing communication between pharmacists, prescribers, and patients is vital. Pharmacists should take the time to counsel patients on their medications, clarify any doubts with prescribers, and ensure that all relevant health information is available before dispensing medication. Clear and open communication helps to prevent misunderstandings and ensures that all parties are aware of potential risks.
5. **Patient Involvement**: Encouraging patients to be active participants in their healthcare can help prevent medication errors. Pharmacists should educate patients on the importance of following their prescribed treatment regimen, understanding their medications, and reporting any side effects or concerns. Patients who are informed and engaged are more likely to adhere to their treatment and avoid errors.

FOUR

Inventory Control in Community Pharmacy

4.1 Definition and Importance of Inventory Control

Inventory control in a community pharmacy refers to the systematic approach to managing the stock of medications and other healthcare products to ensure that the pharmacy operates efficiently, meets customer demand, and minimizes costs. Effective inventory control involves maintaining the right balance of stock—ensuring that the pharmacy has enough medications to meet patient needs without overstocking, which can lead to wastage, especially with products that have expiration dates.

At its core, inventory control is about **managing the flow of goods** into and out of the pharmacy. This process includes ordering medications from suppliers, storing them correctly, tracking their usage, and ensuring that they are dispensed in a timely manner. Proper inventory control helps prevent both stockouts, where a necessary medication is unavailable when needed, and overstocking, which can tie up capital and lead to increased costs due to expired or unused stock.

The **importance of inventory control** in a community pharmacy cannot be overstated. Firstly, it ensures that patients have consistent access to the medications they need. A well-managed inventory means that common and essential medications are always available, and the pharmacy can respond quickly to sudden increases in demand, such as during a flu season or a local outbreak of illness. For example, a pharmacy with good inventory control might anticipate the increased demand for antiviral medications during flu season and stock up accordingly, ensuring that they can meet the needs of their patients without interruption.

Secondly, effective inventory control helps **reduce costs and increase profitability**. By carefully managing stock levels, pharmacies can avoid the financial losses associated with expired medications. Medications that expire before they are sold represent a direct financial loss, as they must be disposed of and cannot be returned to suppliers. Additionally, efficient inventory control can help reduce the costs associated with emergency orders, which are often more expensive due to expedited shipping fees and higher prices for small quantities. For instance, regularly monitoring inventory levels and reordering medications before they run out can help the pharmacy avoid the need for last-minute purchases, which tend to be more costly.

Another critical aspect of inventory control is its role in **regulatory compliance**. Pharmacies are required by law to maintain accurate records of their inventory, especially for controlled substances. These records must be available for inspection by regulatory authorities, and any discrepancies between the recorded inventory and the actual stock can lead to significant legal and financial penalties. For example, a discrepancy in the inventory of a controlled substance like morphine could prompt an investigation by regulatory authorities, leading to fines or even the suspension of the pharmacy's license if the discrepancy cannot be satisfactorily explained.

Inventory control also contributes to **improved patient care**. By ensuring that medications are always available and that stock levels are maintained accurately, pharmacies can provide timely and reliable service to their patients. Patients who receive their medications promptly and without delays are more likely to adhere to their prescribed treatment regimens, leading to better health outcomes. For instance, a patient with a chronic condition such as diabetes who can consistently obtain their insulin from the pharmacy is more likely to maintain stable blood glucose levels, reducing the risk of complications.

Moreover, effective inventory control allows pharmacies to **optimize their storage space**. Pharmacies often have limited storage areas, and by managing their inventory efficiently, they can make the most of the available space. This not only helps in keeping the pharmacy organized but also ensures that medications are stored under the proper conditions, which is critical for maintaining their efficacy. For example, certain medications require refrigeration, and by carefully controlling inventory levels, the pharmacy can ensure that these medications are stored correctly without overcrowding the refrigeration units.

4.2.1 ABC Analysis

ABC analysis is a widely used method of inventory control in community pharmacies, helping to categorize and manage stock based on the value and consumption rate of items. This method is based on the Pareto principle, which states that a small percentage of items in inventory often account for a large percentage of the total value. By classifying inventory into three categories—A, B, and C—pharmacies can prioritize their resources and focus on managing the most critical and valuable items more effectively.

In ABC analysis, **Category A** items are the most valuable products that contribute to the highest portion of the pharmacy's total inventory value, typically around 70-80%. These items are usually high-cost medications or those with a high turnover rate. For example, a community pharmacy might classify expensive biologics or specialty drugs used in chronic conditions like rheumatoid arthritis or multiple sclerosis as Category A items. Because these items represent a significant portion of the pharmacy's investment, they require strict control and frequent monitoring. Stock levels for Category A items are often checked daily or weekly, and reordering processes are closely managed to ensure that these critical medications are always available to meet patient needs.

Category B items are moderately valuable, contributing to about 15-25% of the total inventory value. These items are usually mid-range in cost and have a moderate turnover rate. For instance, common antibiotics, antihypertensives, or diabetic medications might fall into this category. While not as critical as Category A items, Category B items still require regular monitoring, though less frequently—perhaps on a bi-weekly or monthly basis. Inventory management strategies for Category B items might include setting reorder points that trigger replenishment orders before stock levels drop too low, thereby avoiding stockouts without tying up excessive capital in inventory.

Category C items are the least valuable in terms of their contribution to the total inventory value, typically accounting for only 5-10%. These items are usually low-cost and have a low turnover rate. Over-the-counter (OTC) medications, supplements, and basic first-aid supplies often fall into this category. Although these items are less critical to the pharmacy's financial health, they still need to be managed effectively to ensure that the pharmacy can meet all patient needs. Inventory control for Category C items might involve less frequent stock checks, such as monthly or quarterly reviews, and maintaining smaller stock levels to avoid overstocking.

The primary advantage of ABC analysis is that it allows pharmacies to **allocate their resources** more efficiently. By focusing more attention on Category A items, which have the greatest impact on inventory costs, pharmacies can reduce the risk of stockouts for high-value medications, minimize carrying costs, and improve overall inventory turnover. For example, by closely monitoring and managing the inventory of high-cost medications, a pharmacy can reduce the risk of these drugs expiring on the shelf, thereby avoiding significant financial losses.

Additionally, ABC analysis helps in **optimizing ordering processes**. For Category A items, pharmacies might use just-in-time (JIT) ordering to ensure that stock levels are kept low while still meeting patient demand. For Category B and C items, bulk ordering or less frequent replenishment may be more appropriate, helping to reduce ordering and handling costs. By tailoring the ordering process to the specific needs of each category, pharmacies can streamline their operations and reduce unnecessary expenses.

Implementing ABC analysis requires accurate and up-to-date inventory records, as well as an understanding of the pharmacy's sales patterns and the financial impact of each product. The classification should be reviewed periodically to adjust for changes in market demand, medication prices, or the introduction of new products. For example, a medication that was once classified as Category B might move to Category A if its price increases significantly or if it becomes a standard treatment for a newly prevalent condition.

4.2.2 VED Analysis

VED analysis, which stands for Vital, Essential, and Desirable, is another important inventory control method used in community pharmacies. Unlike ABC analysis, which categorizes items based on their financial value, VED analysis focuses on the criticality of the items in terms of patient care. This method helps pharmacies prioritize the stocking of medications and supplies that are vital for patient health, ensuring that critical drugs are always available when needed.

In VED analysis, inventory items are classified into three categories: **Vital**, **Essential**, and **Desirable**.

1. **Vital (V) items** are those that are absolutely necessary for patient survival and treatment. These include life-saving medications and those used in the treatment of acute, severe conditions where any delay in administration could result in significant harm or even death. Examples of vital items in a community pharmacy might include epinephrine auto-injectors (used in severe allergic reactions), insulin (for diabetes), and nitroglycerin tablets (for angina). Because of their critical importance, vital items must always be in stock, and the pharmacy should maintain a higher level of safety stock for these products. Stockouts of vital items can lead to dire consequences, so these items are given the highest priority in inventory management.
2. **Essential (E) items** are those that are important for managing chronic conditions or for preventing the progression of disease, but where a short delay in treatment would not typically result in immediate danger to the patient. These might include antihypertensives, oral hypoglycemics, and common antibiotics. While essential items are important for maintaining patient health, they do not require as high a level of urgency as vital items. However, pharmacies should still ensure that these items are readily available, as prolonged stockouts could lead to worsening of a patient's condition. The inventory strategy for essential items might involve regular monitoring and timely reordering to maintain sufficient stock levels without overstocking.
3. **Desirable (D) items** are those that, while beneficial for patient care, are not critical for survival or the immediate management of health conditions. These items might include vitamins, dietary supplements, and certain over-the-counter (OTC) products that patients might use for general well-being or minor ailments. Desirable items are generally stocked based on consumer demand rather than clinical necessity. Since stockouts of these items do not pose a significant risk to patient health, pharmacies may choose to maintain lower stock levels or reorder them less frequently. Inventory management for desirable items is more flexible, and decisions can be driven by factors such as seasonal demand or promotional sales.

The primary benefit of VED analysis is that it enables pharmacies to **allocate their resources** effectively based on the clinical importance of the products. By ensuring that vital and essential items are always available, pharmacies can provide better care to their patients and prevent adverse health outcomes. For instance, a pharmacy that runs out of insulin, an essential drug for diabetes management, could seriously jeopardize the health of its patients. Therefore, VED analysis helps in prioritizing the procurement and stocking of such critical medications.

VED analysis also plays a crucial role in **emergency preparedness**. In situations such as natural disasters, pandemics, or supply chain disruptions, pharmacies need to have a clear understanding of which items are vital and essential to prioritize their procurement and allocation. For example, during the COVID-19 pandemic, certain medications and supplies became critically important, and VED analysis would have been instrumental in ensuring that these items were adequately stocked.

Implementing VED analysis requires a thorough understanding of the pharmacy's patient population and the specific health needs of the community it serves. The classification of items as vital, essential, or desirable should be based on clinical guidelines, patient demographics, and historical data on the demand for specific medications. Regular reviews and updates to the VED classification are necessary to reflect changes in treatment protocols, emerging health trends, or new medications that may enter the market.

4.2.3 Economic Order Quantity (EOQ)

Economic Order Quantity (EOQ) is a crucial inventory management tool used in community pharmacies to determine the optimal order quantity that minimizes the total cost of inventory. The EOQ model balances the trade-off between the costs associated with ordering and holding inventory, helping pharmacies maintain sufficient stock levels while minimizing expenses. This method is particularly valuable for ensuring that pharmacies operate efficiently, reducing both excess inventory and stockouts.

The EOQ formula is derived from a mathematical model that considers three primary factors: **ordering costs**, **holding costs**, and **demand**.

1. **Ordering Costs** refer to the expenses incurred every time an order is placed. These costs include administrative expenses, shipping fees, and any costs associated with receiving and processing the order. For instance, every time a pharmacy orders a batch of medications, there are fixed costs associated with placing the order, regardless of the size of the order. These costs can accumulate quickly if the pharmacy places frequent small orders, leading to higher overall expenses.

2. **Holding Costs** are the costs associated with storing and maintaining inventory. These costs include warehousing expenses, insurance, spoilage, obsolescence, and the opportunity cost of the capital tied up in inventory. For example, if a pharmacy orders too much stock, it will incur higher holding costs as it needs to store the excess inventory until it is sold. Moreover, medications have expiration dates, so holding too much stock increases the risk of having to discard expired products, resulting in financial losses.
3. **Demand** represents the rate at which the pharmacy expects to sell a particular item. Accurate demand forecasting is essential for calculating the EOQ, as it ensures that the pharmacy orders the right quantity of stock to meet patient needs without overstocking.

The EOQ formula is given by:

$$EOQ = \sqrt{\frac{2DS}{H}}$$

Where:

- D is the annual demand for the product,
- S is the ordering cost per order, and
- H is the holding cost per unit per year.

By using this formula, a pharmacy can determine the most cost-effective quantity of an item to order each time, striking a balance between ordering and holding costs.

Application of EOQ in Community Pharmacy

Implementing EOQ in a community pharmacy involves calculating the optimal order quantity for each medication or product based on the factors outlined above. For example, if a pharmacy typically sells 1,000 units of a particular medication annually, incurs an ordering cost of ₹500 per order, and has a holding cost of ₹10 per unit per year, the EOQ would help determine the ideal order size to minimize costs. In this case, if the EOQ calculation suggests that the pharmacy should order 100 units at a time, this would minimize the total costs associated with ordering and holding the inventory.

EOQ is particularly useful for managing medications with steady demand and predictable sales patterns. For such items, EOQ helps the pharmacy avoid the inefficiencies of overstocking or understocking, ensuring that inventory levels are aligned with patient needs. For instance, if a certain medication is consistently in demand due to its use in chronic disease management, EOQ can help the pharmacy maintain an optimal stock level, reducing the need for frequent reordering while also minimizing holding costs.

Advantages and Limitations of EOQ

The primary advantage of EOQ is its ability to reduce inventory costs by optimizing order quantities. By following the EOQ model, pharmacies can minimize the total cost associated with inventory, freeing up capital for other operational needs. Additionally, EOQ provides a systematic approach to inventory management, reducing the likelihood of stockouts and ensuring that the pharmacy can consistently meet patient demand.

However, there are some limitations to the EOQ model. The EOQ formula assumes that demand, ordering costs, and holding costs are constant, which may not always be the case in a real-world pharmacy setting. Demand for medications can fluctuate due to seasonal variations, changes in patient demographics, or shifts in prescribing patterns. Similarly, ordering costs may vary depending on supplier pricing, shipping fees, or changes in the supply chain. As a result, the EOQ model may need to be adjusted or recalibrated regularly to reflect changing conditions.

Moreover, EOQ is less effective for managing medications with highly variable or unpredictable demand, such as those used in emergency situations or newly launched drugs. In such cases, pharmacies may need to rely on alternative inventory management strategies, such as just-in-time (JIT) ordering or safety stock policies, to ensure that they can respond quickly to changes in demand.

4.2.4 Lead Time and Safety Stock

Lead time and safety stock are critical components of inventory control in community pharmacies, ensuring that the pharmacy can meet patient demand even in the face of supply chain uncertainties. Proper management of lead time and safety stock helps prevent stockouts, which can disrupt patient care, and also reduces the risk of overstocking, which ties up capital and increases storage costs.

Lead time refers to the time it takes from placing an order with a supplier to the time the order is received and available for dispensing. This includes the time required for the supplier to process the order, the transportation time, and the time needed for the pharmacy to receive, check, and store the products. Lead time can vary depending on factors such as the supplier's location, shipping method, and the availability of the ordered items. For instance, a pharmacy that orders medications from a local distributor might have a lead time of just a few days, while orders from international suppliers could take weeks.

Accurately calculating lead time is essential for effective inventory management. If the lead time is underestimated, the pharmacy may run out of stock before the next order arrives, leading to stockouts and potential disruptions in patient care. Conversely, overestimating lead time could result in ordering too early, leading to excess inventory and higher holding costs.

To mitigate the risks associated with lead time variability, pharmacies maintain a **safety stock**—an additional quantity of inventory kept on hand to cover unexpected increases in demand or delays in supply. Safety stock acts as a buffer, ensuring that the pharmacy can continue to meet patient needs even if the actual lead time exceeds expectations or if there is an unforeseen spike in demand. For example, during flu season, a pharmacy might keep extra stock of antiviral medications and flu vaccines to accommodate the higher demand.

The amount of safety stock needed depends on several factors, including the lead time, the variability in demand, and the criticality of the medication. For medications that are vital for patient care, such as insulin or heart medications, pharmacies typically maintain higher levels of safety stock to avoid any risk of stockouts. Conversely, for medications with predictable demand and stable supply chains, the safety stock levels can be lower.

Calculating Safety Stock

Safety stock is generally calculated based on the standard deviation of demand during the lead time, along with a desired service level (the probability of not encountering a stockout). The formula often used is:

Safety Stock=$Z \times \sigma L$

Where:

- Z is the Z-score corresponding to the desired service level (e.g., a 95% service level corresponds to a Z-score of 1.65),
- σL is the standard deviation of demand during the lead time.

For example, if a pharmacy wants to maintain a 95% service level and the standard deviation of demand during the lead time is 50 units, the safety stock required would be approximately 82.5 units (1.65 × 50). This buffer ensures that there is enough stock to cover most variations in demand and lead time.

Optimizing Lead Time and Safety Stock

Pharmacies can optimize lead time and safety stock by regularly reviewing their supply chain processes and working closely with suppliers. Shortening lead time through faster shipping methods or by sourcing from closer suppliers can reduce the need for high levels of safety stock, freeing up capital for other uses. For instance, a pharmacy might negotiate with suppliers for quicker delivery times or establish relationships with multiple suppliers to ensure a more reliable and flexible supply chain.

Additionally, pharmacies should continuously monitor demand patterns and adjust safety stock levels accordingly. During periods of high demand, such as a pandemic or seasonal outbreaks, safety stock levels may need to be increased to prevent stockouts. Conversely, during periods of stable or declining demand, safety stock can be reduced to avoid overstocking.

Impact on Financial Performance

Proper management of lead time and safety stock directly impacts the financial performance of a pharmacy. Holding too much safety stock can increase holding costs, including storage, insurance, and the risk of obsolescence, especially for medications with short shelf lives. On the other hand, insufficient safety stock can lead to stockouts, missed sales, and dissatisfied customers, potentially driving them to competitors. By optimizing lead time and safety stock, pharmacies can strike a balance between minimizing costs and ensuring reliable service to patients.

FIVE

PHARMACEUTICAL CARE

5.1 Definition of Pharmaceutical Care

Pharmaceutical care is a patient-centered approach to pharmacy practice that emphasizes the responsible provision of drug therapy to achieve specific therapeutic outcomes that improve a patient's quality of life. Unlike traditional pharmacy practices that primarily focus on the dispensing of medications, pharmaceutical care encompasses a broader scope of services, including the assessment of medication regimens, monitoring of therapeutic outcomes, and active involvement in the patient's healthcare management.

At its core, pharmaceutical care involves the **collaborative relationship** between the pharmacist, the patient, and other healthcare providers. The pharmacist plays a crucial role in ensuring that the patient receives the most appropriate, effective, and safe medication therapy. This involves not only dispensing the correct medication but also ensuring that the patient understands how to take the medication, monitoring the patient's response to therapy, and making necessary adjustments to the treatment plan in consultation with the prescriber.

The goal of pharmaceutical care is to **optimize medication therapy** to improve patient outcomes. This includes preventing and resolving medication-related problems, such as adverse drug reactions, drug interactions, and issues related to medication adherence. For example, a pharmacist providing pharmaceutical care might identify that a patient is experiencing side effects from a prescribed medication and work with the prescribing physician to adjust the dosage or switch to an alternative therapy that is better tolerated.

Pharmaceutical care also involves the **assessment of the patient's overall health status** and the integration of medication therapy with other aspects of the patient's care. This holistic approach ensures that medication therapy is aligned with the patient's overall health goals and that any potential barriers to effective treatment, such as economic constraints or cognitive limitations, are addressed. For instance, if a patient is unable to afford their prescribed medication, the pharmacist might work with the healthcare team to find a more affordable alternative or assist the patient in accessing financial assistance programs.

One of the key elements of pharmaceutical care is **patient education and empowerment**. Pharmacists play a vital role in educating patients about their medications, including how to take them correctly, the importance of adherence, and what to do if they miss a dose. This education helps empower patients to take an active role in their healthcare, which can lead to better adherence to treatment plans and improved health outcomes. For example, a patient with diabetes might receive detailed counseling on how to use insulin, monitor blood glucose levels, and make lifestyle changes to better manage their condition.

Another important aspect of pharmaceutical care is **medication therapy management (MTM)**, a service that involves a comprehensive review of all the medications a patient is taking. MTM services are particularly beneficial for patients with chronic conditions or those taking multiple medications. Through MTM, the pharmacist assesses the appropriateness of each medication, identifies potential drug interactions, and ensures that the therapy is achieving the desired outcomes. This service not only helps to optimize therapy but also reduces the risk of medication errors and adverse events.

Pharmaceutical care also emphasizes the importance of **continuity of care**. This involves ongoing monitoring of the patient's medication therapy and regular follow-ups to assess the effectiveness of the treatment plan. By maintaining continuous communication with the patient and other healthcare providers, the pharmacist can ensure that any changes in the patient's condition are promptly addressed and that the treatment plan is adjusted as needed. For example, if a patient develops a new health condition or experiences a significant change in their health status, the pharmacist can work with the healthcare team to modify the medication regimen accordingly.

5.2 Principles of Pharmaceutical Care

The principles of pharmaceutical care serve as the foundation for delivering high-quality, patient-centered services in the field of pharmacy. These principles guide pharmacists in their practice, ensuring that they provide optimal medication therapy management and contribute positively to the overall healthcare outcomes of their patients. Understanding and applying these principles is essential for pharmacists who aim to fulfill their role as integral members of the healthcare team.

The first principle of pharmaceutical care is the **commitment to patient welfare**. This principle emphasizes that the primary responsibility of the pharmacist is to ensure the well-being of the patient. Every decision and action taken by the pharmacist should be guided by the goal of improving the patient's health and quality of life. For instance, when a patient presents with a new prescription, the pharmacist's focus should not only be on dispensing the medication but also on assessing whether it is the most appropriate therapy for the patient's condition, considering factors such as potential drug interactions, side effects, and the patient's ability to adhere to the prescribed regimen.

Another key principle is **individualized care**. Pharmaceutical care recognizes that each patient is unique, with specific health needs, preferences, and circumstances that must be considered when designing and managing their medication therapy. This principle involves tailoring the treatment plan to fit the individual patient rather than applying a one-size-fits-all approach. For example, a pharmacist might need to adjust the dosage or formulation of a medication for a patient with renal impairment to ensure that the therapy is both safe and effective. Similarly, if a patient has difficulty swallowing tablets, the pharmacist might recommend an alternative dosage form, such as a liquid or dispersible tablet.

Collaboration and communication are also fundamental principles of pharmaceutical care. Effective pharmaceutical care requires the pharmacist to work closely with other healthcare providers, including doctors, nurses, and specialists, to ensure that the patient receives comprehensive and coordinated care. Communication is key in this collaborative process, as it allows the pharmacist to share important information about the patient's medication therapy, resolve any potential issues, and contribute to the overall treatment plan. For instance, if a pharmacist notices that a prescribed medication could interact negatively with another drug the patient is taking, they must communicate this concern to the prescriber and suggest an alternative therapy if necessary.

Evidence-based practice is another crucial principle. Pharmacists are expected to base their recommendations and decisions on the best available scientific evidence, ensuring that the medications they dispense and the advice they provide are supported by current research and clinical guidelines. This principle helps to ensure that patients receive the most effective and safe treatments available. For example, when counseling a patient on a new medication, the pharmacist should provide information that reflects the latest studies and guidelines, helping the patient make informed decisions about their treatment.

Continuity of care is also an essential principle in pharmaceutical care. This principle emphasizes the importance of ongoing monitoring and follow-up to ensure that the patient's medication therapy remains appropriate and effective over time. Pharmacists must take an active role in tracking the patient's progress, adjusting the treatment plan as needed, and addressing any new issues that arise. For example, if a patient experiences side effects from a medication, the pharmacist should follow up to assess the severity of the symptoms and work with the healthcare team to modify the treatment if necessary.

Patient education and empowerment are integral to the practice of pharmaceutical care. Pharmacists have a responsibility to educate their patients about their medications, including how to take them correctly, what side effects to watch for, and how to manage those side effects if they occur. By providing this education, pharmacists empower patients to take an active role in their healthcare, which can lead to better adherence to treatment plans and improved health outcomes. For instance, a pharmacist might teach a patient with asthma how to use an inhaler correctly, ensuring that the patient receives the full benefit of the medication.

Finally, **ethical practice** underpins all aspects of pharmaceutical care. Pharmacists must adhere to the highest ethical standards in their practice, ensuring that their actions are always in the best interest of the patient. This includes maintaining patient confidentiality, providing unbiased information, and avoiding any conflicts of interest that could compromise patient care. For example, a pharmacist must ensure that their recommendations are based solely on the patient's needs and not influenced by external factors such as financial incentives from pharmaceutical companies.

5.2.1 Patient-Centered Care

Patient-centered care is the cornerstone of pharmaceutical care, reflecting a philosophy that prioritizes the needs, preferences, and values of the patient in all aspects of healthcare delivery. In the context of pharmacy practice, patient-centered care involves tailoring medication therapy and related services to the individual needs of each patient, ensuring that they are actively involved in decisions about their treatment and that their overall well-being is the primary focus.

At the heart of patient-centered care is the principle that the **patient is an active participant** in their healthcare. This approach recognizes that patients are experts in their own lives, and their insights and preferences are valuable in creating a treatment plan that they are more likely to follow. For example, a patient-centered approach might involve discussing the pros and cons of different medication options with the patient, considering factors such as ease of use, cost, and potential side effects. By involving the patient in these decisions, the pharmacist helps to ensure that the chosen therapy aligns with the patient's lifestyle and preferences, which can lead to better adherence and outcomes.

Communication is a key component of patient-centered care. Effective communication involves not only providing information but also listening to the patient's concerns, answering their questions, and ensuring that they fully understand their treatment plan. For instance, when counseling a patient on a new medication, the pharmacist should explain how the medication works, how to take it, what side effects might occur, and what to do if they experience any problems. This communication should be clear, concise, and tailored to the patient's level of understanding, using plain language rather than medical jargon.

Empathy and respect are also central to patient-centered care. Pharmacists must approach each patient with compassion, recognizing their unique circumstances and treating them with dignity. This means being sensitive to the patient's cultural background, beliefs, and values, and adjusting care practices accordingly. For example, if a patient has religious beliefs that affect their use of certain medications, the pharmacist should respect these beliefs and work with the patient and their healthcare team to find an alternative that is acceptable to the patient.

Holistic care is another important aspect of patient-centered care. This involves looking beyond the patient's immediate medical needs to consider their overall well-being, including physical, emotional, and social factors. For instance, a pharmacist might identify that a patient with chronic pain is also experiencing depression, and refer them to a mental health professional for support. By addressing all aspects of the patient's health, the pharmacist can help to improve their quality of life and ensure that their care is truly comprehensive.

Accessibility and continuity of care are also vital in a patient-centered approach. Pharmacists should be readily available to their patients, offering support and guidance whenever needed. This might involve providing extended hours, offering consultations by appointment, or being available for follow-up discussions to monitor the patient's progress. Continuity of care means that the pharmacist maintains an ongoing relationship with the patient, regularly reviewing their medication therapy, adjusting it as needed, and ensuring that any changes in the patient's condition are promptly addressed. For example, if a patient's blood pressure is not well controlled on their current medication, the pharmacist might work with the prescriber to adjust the dosage or try a different medication.

5.2.2 Collaboration with Healthcare Professionals

Collaboration with healthcare professionals is a key principle of pharmaceutical care, reflecting the need for a multidisciplinary approach to patient care. Pharmacists, as medication experts, play a crucial role in the healthcare team, working alongside doctors, nurses, and other healthcare providers to ensure that patients receive comprehensive, coordinated, and effective care. This collaboration enhances the quality of care, improves patient outcomes, and helps to prevent medication-related problems.

The **role of the pharmacist** in a collaborative healthcare environment is multifaceted. Pharmacists contribute their expertise in pharmacotherapy, helping to optimize medication regimens, identify potential drug interactions, and monitor patient responses to therapy. For example, when a physician prescribes a new medication for a patient with multiple chronic conditions, the pharmacist can review the patient's entire medication profile to identify any potential interactions or contraindications. If an issue is identified, the pharmacist can consult with the physician to adjust the treatment plan, ensuring that the patient receives safe and effective care.

Effective communication is the cornerstone of successful collaboration between pharmacists and other healthcare professionals. This communication must be clear, timely, and focused on the patient's best interests. Pharmacists are often in a position to provide valuable insights based on their regular interactions with patients, such as noticing patterns of non-adherence or identifying side effects that the patient may not have reported to their doctor. For instance, if a patient frequently forgets to take their medication, the pharmacist can communicate this to the physician and suggest strategies to improve adherence, such as simplifying the medication regimen or using reminder tools.

Interdisciplinary collaboration is especially important in complex cases where patients have multiple health issues requiring coordinated care. In such cases, pharmacists work closely with the rest of the healthcare team to develop a comprehensive care plan that addresses all aspects of the patient's health. For example, in the management of a patient with diabetes, hypertension, and heart disease, the pharmacist might collaborate with the physician to ensure that the prescribed medications are compatible and that the patient receives proper education on managing their conditions. The pharmacist may also work with a dietitian to provide guidance on dietary modifications that support the patient's overall treatment plan.

Shared decision-making is another critical aspect of collaboration in pharmaceutical care. This approach involves the pharmacist, the patient, and other healthcare providers working together to make informed decisions about the patient's treatment. The pharmacist's role in this process is to provide expert advice on medication therapy, including potential risks and benefits, and to help the patient understand their options. For instance, if a patient is prescribed a medication with significant side effects, the pharmacist might discuss alternative treatments with the healthcare team and the patient, allowing the patient to make an informed choice that aligns with their preferences and values.

Documentation and information sharing are also essential components of collaborative practice. Pharmacists must ensure that all relevant information about the patient's medication therapy is accurately documented and shared with the healthcare team. This includes updating electronic health records (EHRs) with information about new prescriptions, changes to existing therapies, and any adverse drug reactions or issues with adherence. By maintaining accurate and up-to-date records, pharmacists help ensure continuity of care and reduce the risk of errors or omissions in the patient's treatment.

Interprofessional education and training are important for fostering collaboration among healthcare professionals. By participating in joint training sessions, pharmacists and other healthcare providers can develop a better understanding of each other's roles and expertise, leading to more effective teamwork. For example, a pharmacist might attend a continuing education course with physicians and nurses on the management of chronic pain, enabling them to contribute more effectively to the multidisciplinary care of patients with pain management needs.

5.2.3 Continuous Quality Improvement

Continuous Quality Improvement (CQI) is a fundamental principle of pharmaceutical care, emphasizing the ongoing efforts to enhance the quality of services provided to patients. In the context of a community pharmacy, CQI involves systematically evaluating and improving all aspects of pharmacy operations, from medication dispensing and patient counseling to inventory management and collaboration with healthcare professionals. The goal of CQI is to create a culture of excellence where the pharmacy consistently strives to improve patient outcomes, increase efficiency, and reduce errors.

At the heart of CQI is the **commitment to excellence** in patient care. This principle recognizes that there is always room for improvement in the delivery of healthcare services and that even small, incremental changes can lead to significant enhancements in quality. For example, a pharmacy might implement a CQI program to reduce the incidence of dispensing errors. By analyzing past errors, identifying their root causes, and implementing targeted interventions, the pharmacy can improve the accuracy of its dispensing process, thereby enhancing patient safety.

Data-driven decision-making is a key component of CQI. This involves collecting and analyzing data on various aspects of pharmacy operations to identify areas where improvements can be made. For instance, a pharmacy might track the time it takes to fill prescriptions, the rate of medication errors, or patient satisfaction scores. By analyzing this data, the pharmacy can pinpoint specific processes that need improvement and develop strategies to address these issues. For example, if data reveals that patients are frequently waiting too long for their prescriptions, the pharmacy might streamline its workflow or increase staffing during peak hours to reduce wait times.

Employee involvement and training are also critical to the success of CQI initiatives. All members of the pharmacy team, from pharmacists to technicians and support staff, play a role in ensuring the quality of care provided to patients. In a CQI-focused environment, employees are encouraged to identify potential areas for improvement and to participate in the development and implementation of solutions. For example, a pharmacy technician might suggest a more efficient way to organize the inventory to reduce the time it takes to locate medications. Continuous training and professional development are also essential, as they ensure that all staff members have the knowledge and skills needed to contribute to the pharmacy's quality improvement efforts.

Patient feedback is an invaluable resource for CQI. Patients are the ultimate beneficiaries of pharmaceutical care, and their experiences provide critical insights into the effectiveness of the services provided. Pharmacies can gather patient feedback through surveys, suggestion boxes, or direct conversations. For example, if patients frequently report confusion about their medication instructions, the pharmacy might revise its counseling procedures to ensure that patients receive clearer, more comprehensive explanations. By listening to patients and addressing their concerns, pharmacies can improve the quality of care and increase patient satisfaction.

Process standardization is another important aspect of CQI. Standardizing procedures ensures that every patient receives the same high level of care, regardless of which pharmacist or technician handles their prescription. This might involve creating standardized protocols for tasks such as prescription verification, patient counseling, or medication compounding. For instance, a standardized checklist for verifying prescriptions can help ensure that all necessary steps are followed, reducing the risk of errors. Standardization also makes it easier to identify deviations from best practices and implement corrective actions.

Regular auditing and monitoring are essential for sustaining CQI efforts. This involves periodically reviewing the pharmacy's operations to ensure that quality standards are being met and that improvement initiatives are effective. For example, a pharmacy might conduct regular audits of its dispensing process to check for compliance with safety protocols and to identify any new areas for improvement. Monitoring can also involve tracking key performance indicators (KPIs), such as error rates, prescription turnaround times, or patient satisfaction scores. By regularly assessing these metrics, the pharmacy can gauge the effectiveness of its CQI initiatives and make data-driven adjustments as needed.

Adapting to change is a critical element of CQI. The healthcare environment is constantly evolving, with new medications, technologies, and regulations emerging regularly. A pharmacy committed to continuous quality improvement must be flexible and responsive to these changes, ensuring that its practices remain current and effective. For example, as new clinical guidelines are released, the pharmacy must update its protocols and train staff accordingly to ensure that patients receive the most up-to-date care.

SIX

PATIENT COUNSELLING

6.1 Definition and Outcomes of Patient Counselling

Patient counselling is a fundamental component of pharmaceutical care that involves the process of educating and guiding patients about their medications, health conditions, and treatment plans. The primary goal of patient counselling is to empower patients with the knowledge and skills they need to manage their health effectively and to ensure that they adhere to their prescribed medication regimens. By providing comprehensive and personalized information, pharmacists play a crucial role in helping patients understand how to take their medications correctly, recognize potential side effects, and make informed decisions about their healthcare.

Definition of Patient Counselling

Patient counselling can be defined as the interactive process between a pharmacist and a patient (or caregiver) wherein the pharmacist provides essential information and advice about the patient's medications and overall health management. This process is not merely a one-way communication but involves active engagement with the patient, including assessing their understanding, addressing concerns, and ensuring that they feel confident in managing their treatment.

The scope of patient counselling includes explaining the purpose of the prescribed medication, the correct dosage and administration, potential side effects, drug interactions, storage instructions, and the importance of adherence to the treatment plan. For example, when counselling a patient newly diagnosed with hypertension, the pharmacist would explain how the prescribed antihypertensive medication works, the importance of taking it consistently at the same time each day, and what to do if a dose is missed.

Outcomes of Patient Counselling

Effective patient counselling has several positive outcomes that significantly impact patient health and the overall success of the treatment plan.

1. **Improved Medication Adherence**: One of the most critical outcomes of patient counselling is enhanced medication adherence. When patients understand the importance of taking their medications as prescribed, they are more likely to follow the regimen consistently. For instance, a patient who is well-informed about the necessity of completing a full course of antibiotics, even if they start feeling better, is less likely to discontinue the medication prematurely, thereby reducing the risk of antibiotic resistance and treatment failure.
2. **Reduced Risk of Medication Errors**: Patient counselling helps reduce the likelihood of medication errors, such as taking the wrong dosage or using the medication incorrectly. By clearly explaining the correct way to take the medication, including the timing, dosage, and method of administration, pharmacists help patients avoid common mistakes. For example, a patient who understands that their medication should be taken with food to enhance absorption and reduce stomach irritation is less likely to experience side effects or reduced efficacy.
3. **Better Management of Side Effects**: Through patient counselling, pharmacists educate patients about potential side effects and what to do if they occur. This knowledge empowers patients to manage minor side effects on their own or seek medical help when necessary. For instance, if a patient knows that a particular medication may cause dizziness, they can take precautions such as avoiding driving or standing up too quickly, thereby reducing the risk of injury.
4. **Enhanced Patient Satisfaction**: Patients who receive thorough counselling from their pharmacists are more likely to feel satisfied with their care. This satisfaction stems from the patient's confidence in their ability to manage their health and the trust they place in their healthcare providers. For example, a patient who receives clear instructions and feels heard during the counselling session is more likely to view the pharmacy as a valuable resource for their healthcare needs.
5. **Improved Health Outcomes**: Ultimately, the combination of better medication adherence, reduced errors, effective side effect management, and increased patient satisfaction leads to improved health outcomes. When patients take their medications correctly and are aware of how

to manage their health, they are more likely to achieve the desired therapeutic outcomes, such as controlled blood pressure, stabilized blood glucose levels, or effective management of chronic pain.

6. **Empowerment and Patient Autonomy**: Patient counselling promotes empowerment by giving patients the knowledge and tools they need to take control of their health. This empowerment leads to increased patient autonomy, where patients are more involved in their healthcare decisions and are better equipped to discuss their treatment options with their healthcare providers. For instance, a patient who understands the role of lifestyle changes in managing their condition may be more proactive in adopting healthier habits alongside their medication regimen.

6.2 Stages of Patient Counselling

Patient counselling is a structured process that involves several stages, each designed to ensure that the patient fully understands their medication regimen and feels supported in managing their health. These stages include introduction and rapport building, medication information sharing, and closing and follow-up. Each stage is crucial for establishing trust, providing clear information, and ensuring that the patient is confident in their ability to adhere to the treatment plan.

6.2.1 Introduction and Rapport Building

The first stage of patient counselling is introduction and rapport building. This stage is essential for creating a positive and trusting relationship between the pharmacist and the patient. Establishing rapport is the foundation of effective communication and ensures that the patient feels comfortable discussing their health concerns and asking questions.

During the introduction, the pharmacist should greet the patient warmly, introduce themselves, and explain the purpose of the counselling session. For example, the pharmacist might say, "Hello, I'm [Name], your pharmacist. I'd like to take a few minutes to go over your new medication and answer any questions you might have." This approach sets a friendly tone and makes it clear that the pharmacist is there to help.

Building rapport involves more than just a friendly introduction; it also requires active listening, empathy, and respect. The pharmacist should pay close attention to the patient's concerns, body language, and tone of voice, responding with understanding and reassurance. For instance, if a patient expresses anxiety about taking a new medication, the pharmacist should acknowledge these feelings and offer support, saying something like, "I understand that starting a new medication can be worrying. Let's talk through how this medication works and what you can expect, so you feel more comfortable."

Establishing rapport is not just about making the patient feel at ease; it also encourages open communication, which is vital for the success of the counselling session. When patients feel that their concerns are heard and respected, they are more likely to share important information about their health, such as previous experiences with medications or difficulties with adherence.

6.2.2 Medication Information Sharing

The second stage of patient counselling is medication information sharing, where the pharmacist provides the patient with detailed and relevant information about their prescribed medications. This stage is the core of the counselling session and requires the pharmacist to convey information in a clear, concise, and understandable manner.

The pharmacist should begin by explaining the **purpose of the medication**, including how it works and why it has been prescribed. For example, the pharmacist might say, "This medication is an antihypertensive, which means it helps to lower your blood pressure by relaxing your blood vessels." Providing this context helps the patient understand the importance of the medication in managing their condition.

Next, the pharmacist should discuss the **correct dosage and administration** of the medication. This includes when and how to take the medication, whether it should be taken with food, and any specific instructions, such as "Take one tablet in the morning with breakfast." The pharmacist should also explain what to do if a dose is missed, providing clear guidance like, "If you miss a dose, take it as soon as you remember, but skip it if it's almost time for your next dose."

Potential side effects are another critical topic during this stage. The pharmacist should inform the patient about common side effects, how to manage them, and when to seek medical advice. For instance, the pharmacist might say, "Some people experience dizziness when they first start taking this medication. If you feel dizzy, try to sit or lie down until it passes. If it becomes severe or doesn't go away, please contact your doctor."

The pharmacist should also address any **drug interactions** and provide advice on what substances to avoid while taking the medication. This might include foods, beverages, or other medications that could interfere with the treatment. For example, "Avoid drinking grapefruit juice while on this medication, as it can increase the risk of side effects."

Throughout this stage, the pharmacist should encourage the patient to ask questions and clarify any doubts. This interactive approach ensures that the patient fully understands the information and feels confident in managing their medication.

6.2.3 Closing and Follow-Up

The final stage of patient counselling is closing and follow-up. This stage is crucial for reinforcing the information provided and ensuring that the patient knows what to do next.

During the closing, the pharmacist should summarize the key points discussed during the session, such as the purpose of the medication, how to take it, and what side effects to watch for. This summary helps reinforce the information and ensures that the patient leaves the session with a clear understanding of their treatment plan. The pharmacist might say, "Just to recap, take one tablet every morning with food, and be aware of possible dizziness. Don't hesitate to contact us if you have any questions or concerns."

The pharmacist should also encourage the patient to reach out if they have any further questions or experience any issues with their medication. Providing contact information and letting the patient know that follow-up support is available helps build trust and encourages ongoing communication. For example, the pharmacist might say, "If you have any questions or notice anything unusual while taking your medication, please give us a call or stop by the pharmacy. We're here to help."

Follow-up is a critical component of patient counselling, as it allows the pharmacist to monitor the patient's progress and address any issues that arise after the initial counselling session. The pharmacist might schedule a follow-up appointment or phone call to check on the patient's adherence and response to the medication. For instance, "Let's schedule a quick follow-up call in a week to see how you're doing with the new medication and make sure everything is going smoothly."

6.3 Barriers to Effective Counselling

Effective patient counselling is essential for ensuring that patients understand their medication regimens and adhere to their treatment plans. However, several barriers can hinder the effectiveness of counselling sessions, impacting the quality of care provided. Understanding these barriers and finding ways to overcome them is crucial for pharmacists to deliver optimal patient care. Key barriers include language barriers, time constraints, and patient compliance issues.

6.3.1 Language Barriers

Language barriers are one of the most significant challenges in patient counselling, particularly in diverse communities where patients may speak different languages or have varying levels of health literacy. When there is a mismatch between the language spoken by the pharmacist and the patient, it can lead to misunderstandings, miscommunication, and ultimately, medication errors.

Patients who do not fully understand the language used during counselling may have difficulty comprehending instructions on how to take their medication, recognizing potential side effects, or understanding the importance of adherence to their treatment plan. For example, if a pharmacist provides counselling in English to a patient whose primary language is Hindi, the patient may not fully grasp the dosage instructions, leading to improper medication use.

To overcome language barriers, pharmacists can use several strategies. One approach is to provide written materials in the patient's preferred language, such as medication guides, labels, and instructions. Additionally, using visual aids or diagrams can help convey important information, especially when language proficiency is limited. Another effective strategy is to involve a translator or interpreter, either in person or through a telephone service, to facilitate communication between the pharmacist and the patient. In some cases, pharmacists who are proficient in multiple languages may directly counsel patients in their native language, enhancing understanding and compliance.

6.3.2 Time Constraints

Time constraints are another common barrier to effective patient counselling. In busy community pharmacy settings, pharmacists often face high patient volumes, leading to limited time for each counselling session. This can result in rushed or incomplete counselling, where essential information may be overlooked or inadequately explained.

When time is limited, pharmacists may struggle to provide comprehensive counselling, such as discussing the purpose of the medication, potential side effects, drug interactions, and the importance of adherence. For instance, a pharmacist who is pressed for time may focus only on the dosage instructions, neglecting to discuss how the medication interacts with other drugs the patient is taking. This can leave patients with unanswered questions or incomplete understanding, increasing the risk of medication errors or non-adherence.

To address time constraints, pharmacists can prioritize key information during counselling sessions, ensuring that the most critical points are covered even when time is short. Additionally, pharmacies can implement strategies to streamline workflow, such as delegating routine tasks to pharmacy technicians, allowing pharmacists more time for patient counselling. Scheduling appointments for more in-depth counselling sessions or follow-up consultations can also help manage time effectively while ensuring that patients receive the information they need.

6.3.3 Patient Compliance Issues

Patient compliance, or adherence to the prescribed treatment plan, is a major challenge in effective counselling. Even when patients understand the instructions provided during counselling, they may face barriers to compliance, such as forgetfulness, side effects, financial constraints, or lack of motivation.

Non-compliance can result from a variety of factors. For example, a patient may skip doses of their medication because they experience unpleasant side effects or because they believe the medication is unnecessary once they start feeling better. In other cases, patients may have difficulty affording their medications, leading to skipped doses or rationing of their supply. Additionally, patients with chronic conditions may experience "treatment fatigue," where long-term adherence becomes increasingly challenging over time.

To improve compliance, pharmacists can use several approaches. One strategy is to explore the patient's specific barriers to adherence during the counselling session and provide tailored solutions. For example, if a patient struggles with forgetfulness, the pharmacist might suggest using a pill organizer or setting reminders on their phone. If side effects are a concern, the pharmacist can discuss ways to manage them or work with the healthcare provider to adjust the treatment plan.

Financial barriers can be addressed by helping patients access prescription assistance programs, generic alternatives, or more affordable treatment options. Additionally, motivational interviewing techniques can be used to help patients recognize the importance of adherence and take an active role in managing their health.

6.4 Strategies to Overcome Barriers

Effective patient counselling is crucial for ensuring that patients understand their treatment plans and adhere to their medications. However, several barriers can impede the success of counselling sessions, such as language differences, time constraints, and patient compliance issues. To overcome these challenges, pharmacists can employ various strategies, including the use of visual aids and simplified language, to enhance communication and improve patient outcomes.

6.4.1 Use of Visual Aids

Visual aids are powerful tools that can significantly enhance patient understanding during counselling sessions. They help convey complex information in a clear and accessible way, making it easier for patients to grasp key concepts related to their medications and health conditions. Visual aids can include diagrams, charts, pictures, and even videos, which can illustrate how a medication works, the correct way to take it, or the potential side effects to watch for.

For example, a pharmacist might use a diagram of the human body to explain how a medication affects specific organs or systems. This can be particularly useful for patients who have limited literacy skills or who may struggle to understand written or verbal instructions alone. By visually demonstrating the action of a drug, patients are more likely to retain the information and understand its importance.

In addition to diagrams, **pictograms** are another effective visual aid, especially for conveying instructions on medication use. Pictograms are simple, clear images that depict specific actions, such as taking a pill with water, storing medication in a cool place, or avoiding alcohol while on a particular medication. These visuals can be especially helpful for patients who speak different languages or who may not fully understand the pharmacist's verbal instructions. For instance, a pictogram showing a glass of water next to a pill can clearly communicate the need to take the medication with water, regardless of the patient's language proficiency.

Videos and interactive digital tools can also be used as visual aids. These resources can provide dynamic and engaging explanations of how to use certain medical devices, such as inhalers or insulin pens. For instance, a short video demonstrating the correct technique for using an inhaler can be shown to a patient during the counselling session, ensuring that they understand the steps involved. This method can be particularly effective for patients who need to see the process in action to fully grasp it.

By incorporating visual aids into counselling sessions, pharmacists can bridge the gap between complex medical information and the patient's ability to understand and apply that information. This approach not only improves patient comprehension but also enhances their confidence in managing their health, leading to better adherence and outcomes.

6.4.2 Simplified Language

Another essential strategy for overcoming barriers in patient counselling is the use of simplified language. Medical terminology and jargon can be confusing and overwhelming for patients, particularly those with low health literacy or limited education. To ensure that patients fully understand their medication instructions, pharmacists should use clear, straightforward language that is free of technical terms and complex sentence structures.

Simplified language involves breaking down complex concepts into easy-to-understand terms. For example, instead of saying "Take this medication on an empty stomach to ensure optimal absorption," a pharmacist might say, "Take this medicine at least one hour before eating or two hours after eating." This simplified instruction is more likely to be understood by patients, reducing the risk of misunderstandings and errors.

In addition to simplifying the language used during verbal counselling, pharmacists should also apply this approach to written materials, such as medication labels, information leaflets, and patient education brochures. These materials should be written at a level that is accessible to all patients, ideally using language that is no higher than a sixth-grade reading level. For example, a label might say, "Take one tablet by mouth every day" instead of "Administer one oral tablet daily."

Using analogies and examples can also help clarify complex information. For instance, when explaining the importance of taking medication regularly, a pharmacist might compare it to watering a plant: "Just like a plant needs water every day to stay healthy, your body needs this medicine every day to help control your blood pressure." Such comparisons make abstract concepts more relatable and easier to understand.

It is also important for pharmacists to **check for understanding** by asking patients to repeat the instructions in their own words. This technique, known as the "teach-back" method, allows the pharmacist to confirm that the patient has understood the information correctly and provides an opportunity to clarify any points of confusion. For example, after explaining how to use an inhaler, the pharmacist might ask, "Can you show me how you'll use your inhaler at home?" This ensures that the patient knows the correct technique and reinforces the instruction.

6.5 Patient Information Leaflets

Patient information leaflets (PILs) are an essential tool in patient counselling, providing written instructions and information that patients can refer to after their consultation with the pharmacist. These leaflets serve as a valuable resource, reinforcing verbal counselling and ensuring that patients have access to important details about their medications, health conditions, and treatment plans. The effectiveness of a PIL depends on its content, design, layout, and the use of advisory labels, all of which contribute to clear communication and patient understanding.

6.5.1 Content and Design

The content of a patient information leaflet should be comprehensive yet concise, providing all necessary information in a format that is easy for patients to understand. The primary goal of the content is to educate patients about their medications, including how to take them, what to expect, and how to manage any potential side effects. The leaflet should cover several key areas:

1. **Medication Name and Purpose**: The leaflet should clearly state the name of the medication (both brand and generic names) and explain its purpose. For example, "This medication is used to lower blood pressure and reduce the risk of heart attacks and strokes."
2. **Dosage and Administration Instructions**: Detailed instructions on how to take the medication should be included, such as the correct dosage, timing, and method of administration. For instance, "Take one tablet by mouth every morning with water, with or without food."
3. **Possible Side Effects**: The leaflet should list common side effects, what to do if they occur, and when to seek medical attention. For example, "You may experience dizziness or headache. If you notice severe side effects such as chest pain or difficulty breathing, contact your doctor immediately."
4. **Drug Interactions and Precautions**: Information about potential drug interactions and any precautions the patient should take is also critical. For example, "Avoid taking this medication with grapefruit juice, as it may increase the risk of side effects."
5. **Storage Instructions**: Proper storage instructions help ensure the medication remains effective. For example, "Store in a cool, dry place

away from direct sunlight."

6. **Contact Information**: The leaflet should include the pharmacy's contact information in case the patient has further questions or needs additional assistance.

When designing the content, it is important to use **clear and simple language** that is free of medical jargon. The information should be presented at a reading level that is accessible to the majority of patients, ideally around a sixth-grade level. Additionally, the content should be organized logically, with headings and subheadings that guide the reader through the information.

6.5.2 Layouts and Advisory Labels

The layout of a patient information leaflet is just as important as its content. A well-designed layout ensures that the information is easy to navigate and visually appealing, which can enhance patient comprehension and retention. The following elements should be considered in the layout design:

1. **Clear Headings and Subheadings**: Using bold and descriptive headings helps to organize the information and allows patients to quickly find the sections they need. For example, headings like "How to Take Your Medication" and "Possible Side Effects" guide the reader through the leaflet.
2. **Bullet Points and Numbered Lists**: Breaking down information into bullet points or numbered lists makes it easier to read and understand. This is particularly useful for instructions or lists of side effects, where clarity is essential.
3. **Font Size and Style**: The font should be large enough to be easily readable, typically at least 12-point size, and in a simple, clear typeface like Arial or Times New Roman. Avoid using overly decorative fonts that may be difficult to read.
4. **Use of White Space**: Adequate white space around text and between sections helps prevent the leaflet from appearing cluttered and overwhelming. It also makes the content easier to scan and read.
5. **Images and Diagrams**: Incorporating images, diagrams, or pictograms can be very effective in enhancing understanding, especially for patients with low literacy levels. For example, a diagram showing how to use an inhaler or an image indicating the correct way to apply a topical cream

can reinforce the written instructions.

Advisory labels are additional tools that can be included in or attached to patient information leaflets. These labels provide specific warnings or instructions that are crucial for the safe and effective use of the medication. Examples of advisory labels include:

- **"Do not drive or operate machinery after taking this medication"**: This warning is important for medications that can cause drowsiness or impair coordination.
- **"Take with food or milk"**: This label helps prevent gastrointestinal discomfort that can occur with certain medications.
- **"Store in the refrigerator"**: This advisory ensures that the medication is stored at the correct temperature to maintain its efficacy.

These labels should be prominently displayed on the leaflet or medication packaging, using bold colors and symbols to draw attention. For example, a bright yellow label with a caution symbol can alert patients to important safety information.

SEVEN

PATIENT MEDICATION ADHERENCE

7.1 Definition of Medication Adherence

Medication adherence refers to the extent to which a patient correctly follows their prescribed medication regimen. It encompasses the patient's ability to take the right dose, at the right time, in the prescribed manner, and for the prescribed duration. Medication adherence is a crucial factor in the effectiveness of treatment plans, as it directly influences the outcomes of therapy. Poor adherence can lead to suboptimal therapeutic outcomes, worsening of the condition, increased healthcare costs, and even the development of drug resistance, particularly in chronic conditions like hypertension, diabetes, and HIV.

The term **adherence** is often used interchangeably with **compliance**, but it is important to note the subtle difference between the two. Compliance generally refers to the patient's passive following of the healthcare provider's instructions, while adherence implies a more active, collaborative process where the patient is involved in making informed decisions about their treatment. Adherence recognizes the patient's role in managing their health and emphasizes the importance of patient education, motivation, and empowerment.

Several factors influence medication adherence, including the complexity of the medication regimen, the patient's understanding of their condition and the importance of the medication, side effects, cost of medication, and the patient's relationship with their healthcare provider. For example, a patient prescribed a complex regimen involving multiple medications taken at different times throughout the day may find it challenging to adhere to the schedule, leading to missed doses or incorrect administration. Similarly, if a patient experiences unpleasant side effects or perceives no immediate benefit from the medication, they may be less motivated to continue taking it as prescribed.

Medication adherence is often measured in terms of **medication possession ratio (MPR)** or **proportion of days covered (PDC)**, which assess the consistency with which a patient obtains and uses their medication. These metrics are useful for identifying patterns of non-adherence, such as frequently missed doses or premature discontinuation of therapy. For instance, if a patient's PDC is below 80%, it indicates that they are not consistently taking their medication as prescribed, which could compromise the effectiveness of their treatment.

Improving medication adherence is a shared responsibility between the patient and the healthcare provider, particularly the pharmacist. Pharmacists play a key role in supporting adherence by providing patient education, simplifying medication regimens when possible, offering reminders or tools to help patients remember their doses, and addressing any barriers to adherence, such as side effects or financial constraints. For example, a pharmacist might suggest using a pill organizer for a patient who struggles with remembering to take their medication or discuss alternative medications if cost is a barrier.

7.2 Factors Affecting Medication Adherence

Medication adherence is influenced by a wide range of factors that can either support or hinder a patient's ability to follow their prescribed treatment regimen. These factors are often complex and interrelated, impacting the patient's willingness and ability to take their medications as directed. Two significant categories of factors that affect medication adherence are socioeconomic factors and medication-related factors.

7.2.1 Socioeconomic Factors

Socioeconomic factors play a crucial role in determining a patient's ability to adhere to their medication regimen. These factors include income level, education, employment status, and social support, all of which can significantly impact a patient's access to medications and their ability to follow prescribed treatments.

One of the most critical socioeconomic factors is **financial constraints**. Patients with lower income levels may struggle to afford their medications, leading to non-adherence due to the high cost of prescriptions. For example, a patient with limited financial resources might decide to skip doses, halve their medication, or avoid refilling a prescription to save money. This practice can lead to suboptimal therapeutic outcomes and an increased risk of complications. Additionally, patients may prioritize other basic needs, such as food or housing, over purchasing their medications, further exacerbating non-adherence.

Educational level is another important socioeconomic factor. Patients with lower levels of education may have difficulty understanding complex medical instructions or the importance of adhering to their medication regimen. For instance, a patient who is not fully literate may struggle to read and comprehend medication labels, leading to incorrect dosage or administration. Moreover, patients with limited health literacy may not fully understand the implications of non-adherence, such as the potential for disease progression or the development of resistance in cases like antibiotic treatment.

Employment status also affects medication adherence. Patients who are unemployed or have unstable jobs may lack health insurance, making it difficult for them to afford medications. Conversely, patients with demanding jobs or irregular work hours may find it challenging to adhere to a strict medication schedule, particularly if their regimen requires taking medication multiple times a day or at specific times.

Social support is another critical factor. Patients with strong social support networks, including family, friends, or caregivers, are more likely to adhere to their medication regimens. Supportive individuals can help remind patients to take their medications, assist with managing complex regimens, and provide emotional support during treatment. For example, an elderly patient with a caregiver who helps organize and administer medications is more likely to adhere to the prescribed regimen compared to someone who lives alone and lacks such support.

Cultural factors also play a role in medication adherence. Cultural beliefs and practices can influence how patients perceive their illness and treatment. For instance, some patients may rely on traditional remedies or have misconceptions about modern medications, leading to reluctance or refusal to adhere to prescribed treatments. Understanding and addressing these cultural factors through culturally sensitive counselling can help improve adherence.

7.2.2 Medication-Related Factors

Medication-related factors are directly tied to the characteristics of the prescribed drugs and how these factors affect patient adherence. These include the complexity of the medication regimen, side effects, the form of the medication, and the patient's perception of the medication's efficacy.

One of the most significant medication-related factors is **regimen complexity**. Patients who are prescribed complex regimens involving multiple medications, different dosages, and various administration times are more likely to experience difficulties with adherence. For example, a patient with chronic conditions like diabetes, hypertension, and heart disease may be prescribed several medications with different dosing schedules. Keeping track of these medications can be overwhelming, leading to missed doses or incorrect administration. Simplifying the regimen, when possible, by using combination therapies or adjusting dosing schedules, can help improve adherence.

Side effects are another major factor that can deter patients from adhering to their medication regimen. Medications that cause unpleasant or severe side effects, such as nausea, dizziness, or fatigue, may lead patients to discontinue their use or take them irregularly. For instance, a patient taking a medication that causes significant gastrointestinal discomfort may decide to stop taking it altogether, particularly if they do not perceive an immediate benefit from the medication. Effective management of side effects, through dose adjustment or switching to alternative therapies, can help improve adherence.

The **form of the medication** also influences adherence. Patients may have preferences for certain forms of medication, such as tablets, capsules, liquids, or injections. If the prescribed form is difficult for the patient to use, such as large tablets that are hard to swallow or injections that cause pain, they may be less likely to adhere to the treatment. For example, a patient who has difficulty swallowing pills may be more adherent if the medication is available in a liquid form or as a dispersible tablet. Pharmacists can play a crucial role in identifying these preferences and working with healthcare providers to select the most suitable form of medication for the patient.

Perceived efficacy of the medication is another critical factor. Patients are more likely to adhere to their medication regimen if they believe that the medication is effective in managing their condition. However, if patients do not notice immediate improvements or if the medication is for a condition that is asymptomatic, such as high blood pressure, they may question the necessity of the medication and become non-adherent. For example, a patient with hypertension might stop taking their antihypertensive medication if they do not feel any different after taking it, despite the medication working to control their blood pressure.

7.3 Role of Pharmacist in Improving Adherence

Pharmacists play a crucial role in improving medication adherence, ensuring that patients follow their prescribed treatment regimens accurately and consistently. By employing effective counselling techniques and engaging in follow-up and monitoring, pharmacists can address the barriers to adherence, educate patients, and support them in managing their medications effectively. This proactive involvement by pharmacists is essential in enhancing patient outcomes and ensuring the success of therapeutic interventions.

7.3.1 Counseling Techniques

Effective counselling is one of the most important tools pharmacists have to improve medication adherence. Through personalized and patient-centered counselling techniques, pharmacists can educate patients about their medications, address their concerns, and empower them to take an active role in managing their health.

One key counselling technique is the **use of clear and simple language**. Pharmacists should avoid medical jargon and explain medication instructions in terms that are easy for the patient to understand. For instance, instead of saying, "Take this medication BID," the pharmacist should say, "Take one tablet twice a day—once in the morning and once in the evening." This approach ensures that patients fully comprehend how to take their medications correctly, reducing the risk of errors and non-adherence.

Another important technique is **active listening**. By listening attentively to the patient's concerns, pharmacists can identify specific barriers to adherence, such as fear of side effects, financial difficulties, or misunderstandings about the medication's purpose. For example, if a patient expresses worry about potential side effects, the pharmacist can address these concerns by explaining how to manage them or by discussing alternative medications with fewer side effects. Active listening also helps build rapport and trust, making patients more likely to follow the pharmacist's advice.

Motivational interviewing is another effective counselling technique. This approach involves engaging the patient in a collaborative conversation to explore their motivations for taking their medication and to address any ambivalence or resistance. For example, a pharmacist might ask a patient, "What are your goals for managing your diabetes, and how do you think this medication can help you achieve them?" By focusing on the patient's goals and motivations, the pharmacist can help the patient see the importance of adherence in achieving better health outcomes.

Pharmacists can also use **visual aids** and **demonstrations** during counselling sessions. For instance, when counselling a patient on the use of an inhaler, the pharmacist might demonstrate the correct technique using a placebo inhaler. Visual aids, such as diagrams or pictograms, can help reinforce verbal instructions and make complex information more accessible. This is particularly useful for patients with low literacy levels or those who are visual learners.

Teach-back is another valuable technique that involves asking the patient to repeat the instructions in their own words. This helps ensure that the patient has understood the information correctly and provides an opportunity for the pharmacist to clarify any misunderstandings. For example, after explaining how to take a medication, the pharmacist might say, "Just to make sure I've explained everything clearly, can you tell me how you're going to take this medication?"

Personalizing the counselling session to the patient's individual needs and circumstances is also crucial. For example, if a patient is taking multiple medications, the pharmacist might provide a customized medication schedule or recommend the use of a pill organizer to help the patient manage their regimen more effectively. Tailoring the counselling to the patient's lifestyle and preferences increases the likelihood of adherence.

7.3.2 Follow-Up and Monitoring

Follow-up and monitoring are essential components of the pharmacist's role in improving medication adherence. These activities involve ongoing communication with the patient to assess their progress, address any emerging issues, and reinforce the importance of adherence.

Regular follow-up allows the pharmacist to check on the patient's adherence and to identify any problems that may have arisen since the initial counselling session. For example, the pharmacist might schedule a follow-up phone call or appointment a week after the patient starts a new medication to ask, "How are you feeling since you started this medication? Are you experiencing any side effects, or have you had any difficulties taking it as prescribed?" This follow-up helps catch potential adherence issues early and provides an opportunity to make necessary adjustments to the treatment plan.

Monitoring involves tracking the patient's medication use over time. Pharmacists can use tools such as medication possession ratio (MPR) or proportion of days covered (PDC) to assess whether the patient is consistently refilling their prescriptions and taking their medications as directed. For example, if a patient's PDC is below 80%, the pharmacist might reach out to discuss any challenges the patient is facing and explore solutions to improve adherence.

Collaborating with other healthcare providers is another important aspect of follow-up and monitoring. Pharmacists should communicate with the patient's doctors, nurses, and other healthcare professionals to ensure a coordinated approach to care. For instance, if a patient reports side effects or difficulty adhering to their medication regimen, the pharmacist might discuss these issues with the prescribing physician to consider adjusting the treatment plan. This collaboration helps ensure that the patient receives comprehensive and consistent support from the entire healthcare team.

Pharmacists can also use **technology** to enhance follow-up and monitoring efforts. For example, automated phone calls, text message reminders, or mobile apps can be used to remind patients to take their medications or to refill their prescriptions. These tools can help improve adherence by providing regular prompts and making it easier for patients to stay on track with their treatment.

EIGHT

Health Screening Services in Community Pharmacy

8.1 Definition and Importance of Health Screening

Health screening in the community pharmacy setting refers to the process of conducting routine tests or assessments to identify individuals who may be at risk of developing certain health conditions or those who may already have undiagnosed conditions. These screenings are typically non-invasive, quick, and convenient, making them accessible to a wide range of patients. The primary goal of health screening is to detect potential health issues early, allowing for timely intervention, management, and referral to other healthcare providers if necessary.

Health screening services offered in community pharmacies can include blood pressure monitoring, blood glucose testing, cholesterol checks, body mass index (BMI) assessments, and osteoporosis screening, among others. These services are designed to identify risk factors for chronic diseases such as hypertension, diabetes, cardiovascular disease, and osteoporosis, which are prevalent in the general population.

The importance of health screening in community pharmacy cannot be overstated. One of the most significant benefits is the early detection of diseases. Many chronic conditions, such as hypertension and diabetes, often have no noticeable symptoms in their early stages. As a result, individuals may be unaware that they have these conditions until they experience complications. For example, a patient might discover during a routine blood pressure check at a pharmacy that they have hypertension, a condition that could lead to serious complications like stroke or heart attack if left unmanaged. Early detection through health screening enables patients to take proactive steps to manage their health, such as lifestyle modifications or initiating medication therapy, thereby reducing the risk of severe outcomes.

Health screenings in community pharmacies also play a crucial role in **increasing access to healthcare**. Pharmacies are often more accessible than other healthcare facilities, with longer operating hours and no need for appointments. This accessibility makes it easier for individuals, particularly those who may not regularly visit a doctor, to receive important health screenings. For example, individuals who do not have a primary care physician or who may find it difficult to take time off work to visit a doctor can benefit from the convenience of pharmacy-based screenings. By offering these services, community pharmacies help bridge gaps in healthcare access, especially in underserved areas where healthcare resources may be limited.

Another important aspect of health screening is **patient education and empowerment**. During the screening process, pharmacists have the opportunity to educate patients about their health, explain the results of the screenings, and provide advice on how to manage or reduce risk factors. For instance, if a patient's cholesterol levels are high, the pharmacist can discuss dietary changes, the importance of physical activity, and the potential need for medication. This education empowers patients to take control of their health and make informed decisions about their lifestyle and treatment options.

Health screenings also contribute to **public health initiatives** by identifying individuals who may be at risk of communicable diseases or other health concerns that have broader societal implications. For example, during flu season, community pharmacies may offer influenza screenings and vaccinations, helping to reduce the spread of the virus within the community. Similarly, pharmacies may participate in public health campaigns by offering screenings for conditions like HIV or hepatitis, contributing to early detection and prevention efforts.

Moreover, health screening services in community pharmacies can lead to **improved patient outcomes** through the coordination of care. When a screening identifies a potential health issue, pharmacists can refer patients to their primary care physician or a specialist for further evaluation and treatment. This coordinated approach ensures that patients receive comprehensive care and that no potential health issues are overlooked. For instance, a patient who is found to have high blood glucose levels during a pharmacy screening can be referred to an endocrinologist for further assessment and management, helping to prevent the progression of diabetes.

8.2.1 Blood Pressure Measurement

Blood pressure measurement is one of the most common and essential health screening methods offered in community pharmacies. It is a quick, non-invasive procedure that provides critical information about a patient's cardiovascular health. High blood pressure, or hypertension, is often referred to as a "silent killer" because it typically has no symptoms, yet it significantly increases the risk of heart disease, stroke, and other serious health conditions. Regular monitoring of blood pressure is crucial for early detection and management of hypertension.

The process of measuring blood pressure in a community pharmacy setting involves the use of an automated blood pressure monitor or a manual sphygmomanometer. Automated devices are more commonly used in pharmacies due to their ease of use, accuracy, and the ability to quickly obtain readings without extensive training. However, manual sphygmomanometers can also be used, particularly when a more precise measurement is required or when the automated device yields an abnormal result.

Procedure for Blood Pressure Measurement

When a patient arrives for a blood pressure screening, the pharmacist or trained pharmacy staff will typically follow these steps:

1. **Preparation**: The patient is asked to sit quietly for five minutes in a chair with their feet flat on the floor and their back supported. It is important that the patient is relaxed, as stress or recent physical activity can temporarily elevate blood pressure readings. The patient's arm should be positioned at heart level, resting on a table or armrest.
2. **Cuff Placement**: The blood pressure cuff is wrapped snugly around the patient's upper arm, with the lower edge of the cuff placed about an inch above the elbow. The cuff must fit properly to ensure an accurate reading; an incorrectly sized cuff can lead to false readings. For example, a cuff

that is too small may give a falsely high reading, while a cuff that is too large may give a falsely low reading.

3. **Taking the Measurement**: If using an automated device, the machine will inflate the cuff and gradually release the pressure while measuring the systolic and diastolic blood pressure. The systolic pressure, the first number in a blood pressure reading, represents the pressure in the arteries when the heart beats. The diastolic pressure, the second number, represents the pressure in the arteries when the heart is at rest between beats. The machine will display the readings, and some devices may also measure the pulse rate.

If using a manual sphygmomanometer, the pharmacist will inflate the cuff while listening with a stethoscope placed over the brachial artery at the elbow. As the cuff is slowly deflated, the pharmacist listens for the first sound of blood flow (the systolic pressure) and the point at which the sound disappears (the diastolic pressure).

1. **Interpreting the Results**: Once the blood pressure measurement is obtained, the pharmacist will interpret the results and discuss them with the patient. Blood pressure readings are typically classified as follows:

   - **Normal**: Systolic less than 120 mm Hg and diastolic less than 80 mm Hg.
   - **Elevated**: Systolic between 120-129 mm Hg and diastolic less than 80 mm Hg.
   - **Hypertension Stage 1**: Systolic between 130-139 mm Hg or diastolic between 80-89 mm Hg.
   - **Hypertension Stage 2**: Systolic 140 mm Hg or higher or diastolic 90 mm Hg or higher.
   - **Hypertensive Crisis**: Systolic higher than 180 mm Hg and/or diastolic higher than 120 mm Hg, which requires immediate medical attention.

2. **Counseling and Referral**: Depending on the results, the pharmacist will provide counseling on lifestyle modifications, such as diet and exercise, to help manage blood pressure. If the reading indicates hypertension or a hypertensive crisis, the pharmacist will refer the patient to their primary care physician or an emergency department for further evaluation and treatment.

Importance of Blood Pressure Measurement in Community Pharmacy

Regular blood pressure measurement in community pharmacies is crucial for several reasons. First, it allows for the early detection of hypertension, enabling timely intervention and management. Early management of high blood pressure can significantly reduce the risk of complications such as heart attack, stroke, and kidney disease. For example, a patient who discovers that they have elevated blood pressure during a routine pharmacy screening can take steps to lower their blood pressure through lifestyle changes or medication, thereby reducing their risk of cardiovascular events.

Second, blood pressure measurement in pharmacies increases access to healthcare. Many individuals may not visit their doctor regularly but are more likely to visit a pharmacy for various reasons, such as filling prescriptions or purchasing over-the-counter medications. Offering blood pressure screenings in this accessible setting helps identify individuals at risk who might otherwise go undiagnosed.

Finally, blood pressure measurement provides an opportunity for pharmacists to engage in patient education and promote overall cardiovascular health. Pharmacists can discuss the importance of maintaining a healthy blood pressure, provide tips on lifestyle changes that can lower blood pressure, and encourage patients to monitor their blood pressure regularly.

8.2.2 Blood Sugar Testing

Blood sugar testing is a crucial health screening service offered in community pharmacies, particularly for the early detection and management of diabetes. This screening involves measuring the glucose level in the blood, providing essential information about the patient's metabolic health. Diabetes, characterized by chronic hyperglycemia, is a growing public health concern, and early detection through regular blood sugar testing is vital in preventing the progression of the disease and its associated complications.

Blood sugar testing in community pharmacies is typically performed using a small, portable device called a glucometer. This device provides a quick and accurate measurement of blood glucose levels, making it an ideal tool for routine screening in a convenient setting.

Procedure for Blood Sugar Testing

The process of blood sugar testing in a pharmacy setting generally involves the following steps:

1. **Preparation**: The patient is usually asked whether they have fasted or recently eaten, as this can affect the blood sugar reading. Fasting blood glucose tests require the patient to abstain from eating or drinking anything other than water for at least eight hours prior to the test. For random or postprandial (after eating) glucose tests, this is not necessary.
2. **Sample Collection**: The pharmacist or trained staff member will use a lancet to prick the patient's fingertip, obtaining a small drop of blood. This step is quick and minimally invasive, causing only a brief moment of discomfort.
3. **Measuring Blood Sugar**: The drop of blood is placed on a test strip, which is then inserted into the glucometer. The device analyzes the blood sample and provides a reading of the blood glucose level within a few seconds. The results are displayed on the device's screen, showing the patient's blood sugar level in milligrams per deciliter (mg/dL).
4. **Interpreting the Results**: The pharmacist will interpret the blood sugar reading based on the type of test performed:

   - **Fasting Blood Sugar**: A normal fasting blood sugar level is typically between 70 and 99 mg/dL. Levels between 100 and 125 mg/dL may indicate prediabetes, while a level of 126 mg/dL or higher suggests diabetes.
   - **Random Blood Sugar**: A normal random blood sugar level is usually less than 140 mg/dL. Levels between 140 and 199 mg/dL may indicate prediabetes, while levels of 200 mg/dL or higher can suggest diabetes.
   - **Postprandial Blood Sugar**: Blood sugar levels are measured about two hours after eating. A normal level is usually less than 140 mg/dL, while a level between 140 and 199 mg/dL may indicate prediabetes, and 200 mg/dL or higher may suggest diabetes.

5. **Counseling and Referral**: After interpreting the results, the pharmacist will discuss the findings with the patient. If the blood sugar levels are elevated, the pharmacist may advise the patient on lifestyle changes, such as diet and exercise, to help manage their blood sugar. If the levels are significantly high, the pharmacist will refer the patient to their primary care physician or an endocrinologist for further evaluation and possible diagnosis of diabetes.

Importance of Blood Sugar Testing in Community Pharmacy

Blood sugar testing in community pharmacies plays a critical role in the early detection of diabetes, a condition that often goes undiagnosed until complications arise. Regular screening allows for the identification of individuals at risk for diabetes, enabling early intervention and management. For instance, a patient with elevated blood sugar levels detected during a routine screening can be counseled on lifestyle modifications and referred for further testing, potentially preventing the progression to full-blown diabetes.

In addition to early detection, blood sugar testing in pharmacies increases **access to care**. Many individuals may not regularly visit a doctor, either due to time constraints, cost, or lack of awareness. However, they may visit a pharmacy for other needs, presenting an opportunity for screening that they might not otherwise pursue. By offering blood sugar testing, community pharmacies help reach a broader population, particularly those who are underserved or at high risk for diabetes.

Blood sugar testing also provides an opportunity for **patient education**. Pharmacists can educate patients on the importance of maintaining healthy blood sugar levels and the long-term implications of uncontrolled diabetes, such as cardiovascular disease, kidney damage, and neuropathy. For example, a pharmacist might explain how a diet high in refined sugars and low in fiber can contribute to elevated blood sugar levels and suggest dietary changes to help manage or reduce the risk of diabetes.

Moreover, blood sugar testing allows for **ongoing monitoring** of individuals with known diabetes. Patients can regularly check their blood sugar levels in the pharmacy, enabling better management of their condition. This is particularly useful for patients who may have difficulty accessing other healthcare facilities for routine monitoring. For instance, a patient managing type 2 diabetes can have their blood sugar levels checked regularly at the pharmacy, allowing for adjustments to their medication or lifestyle as needed.

8.2.3 Lung Function Tests

Lung function tests are an important component of health screening services offered in community pharmacies, particularly for individuals with respiratory conditions such as asthma, chronic obstructive pulmonary disease (COPD), or those at risk due to smoking or environmental exposure. These tests assess how well the lungs are working by measuring the volume of air a person can inhale and exhale, as well as how quickly air can be expelled from the lungs. Lung function tests provide valuable information that can help in the early detection and management of respiratory conditions.

In a community pharmacy setting, the most common lung function test conducted is **spirometry**. Spirometry is a simple, non-invasive test that measures the amount of air a person can breathe in and out, and how fast they can exhale. The results of a spirometry test can help identify conditions such as asthma, COPD, and other disorders that affect breathing.

Procedure for Lung Function Tests (Spirometry)

The process of conducting a spirometry test in a pharmacy typically involves the following steps:

1. **Preparation**: The patient is asked to sit comfortably and breathe normally for a few minutes. The pharmacist or trained staff member will explain the procedure to the patient, ensuring they understand how to perform the test correctly. It is important that the patient is relaxed and follows the instructions closely to obtain accurate results.
2. **Using the Spirometer**: The patient is instructed to take a deep breath in, filling their lungs completely. They are then asked to place their mouth around the mouthpiece of the spirometer, creating a tight seal with their lips. The patient must then exhale forcefully and as quickly as possible into the spirometer, emptying their lungs completely. This maneuver is usually repeated several times to ensure consistency and accuracy of the results.
3. **Measuring Lung Function**: The spirometer records various measurements during the test, including:
    - **Forced Vital Capacity (FVC)**: The total amount of air exhaled during the test. It measures the volume of air a person can forcefully exhale after taking a deep breath.
    - **Forced Expiratory Volume in 1 Second (FEV1)**: The amount of air exhaled in the first second of the FVC test. FEV1 is a key indicator of lung function and is used to assess the severity of respiratory conditions like asthma and COPD.
    - **FEV1/FVC Ratio**: This ratio compares the amount of air exhaled in the first second to the total amount exhaled. A lower-than-normal ratio can indicate obstructive airway conditions such as asthma or COPD.

4. **Interpreting the Results**: The pharmacist or healthcare provider will interpret the results of the spirometry test based on standard reference values that take into account the patient's age, sex, height, and ethnicity. Normal values for FVC and FEV1 vary, but a healthy individual typically has an FEV1/FVC ratio of around 70-80%. Lower values may indicate obstructive lung diseases.
5. **Counseling and Referral**: Depending on the results, the pharmacist will provide counseling to the patient. If the test indicates the possibility of a respiratory condition, the pharmacist may advise the patient on lifestyle changes, such as quitting smoking or avoiding environmental triggers, and refer them to a pulmonologist or their primary care physician for further evaluation and diagnosis. For instance, if a patient's spirometry results suggest COPD, the pharmacist will recommend a follow-up with a specialist for confirmation and potential initiation of treatment.

Importance of Lung Function Tests in Community Pharmacy

Lung function tests, particularly spirometry, are valuable tools in the early detection and management of respiratory conditions. Many lung diseases, such as asthma and COPD, can develop gradually and may not be diagnosed until significant lung damage has occurred. Regular screening through spirometry allows for the early identification of these conditions, enabling timely intervention and treatment.

For example, a smoker who undergoes regular spirometry testing at their community pharmacy might be diagnosed with early-stage COPD before they experience severe symptoms. Early detection allows for interventions that can slow the progression of the disease, such as smoking cessation programs and the use of bronchodilators.

In addition to early detection, spirometry provides a way to **monitor existing respiratory conditions**. Patients with diagnosed asthma or COPD can use spirometry to track their lung function over time, helping to assess the effectiveness of their treatment and make adjustments as needed. For instance, if a patient's spirometry results show a decline in lung function, the pharmacist can recommend a review of their treatment plan with their healthcare provider.

Lung function tests also serve as an educational opportunity for pharmacists to engage patients in discussions about their respiratory health. Pharmacists can provide advice on how to manage symptoms, avoid triggers, and adhere to prescribed inhaler regimens. For instance, a pharmacist might demonstrate the correct use of an inhaler to a patient with asthma, ensuring they receive the full therapeutic benefit.

8.2.4 Cholesterol Testing

Cholesterol testing is a vital health screening service provided in community pharmacies, playing a key role in the early detection and management of cardiovascular diseases. Cholesterol is a type of fat found in the blood that is essential for the production of cell membranes, hormones, and vitamin D. However, when cholesterol levels are too high, it can lead to the buildup of fatty deposits in the arteries, increasing the risk of heart disease, stroke, and other cardiovascular conditions. Regular cholesterol testing helps individuals monitor their lipid levels and take necessary actions to maintain heart health.

In a community pharmacy setting, cholesterol testing is typically conducted using a small, portable device known as a lipid analyzer. This device provides a quick and accurate measurement of the patient's cholesterol levels, often including total cholesterol, low-density lipoprotein (LDL) cholesterol, high-density lipoprotein (HDL) cholesterol, and triglycerides. These measurements give a comprehensive picture of the patient's lipid profile and help assess their risk for cardiovascular diseases.

Procedure for Cholesterol Testing

The process of conducting a cholesterol test in a pharmacy usually involves the following steps:

1. **Preparation**: The patient may be asked whether they have fasted prior to the test, as fasting can influence the accuracy of certain lipid measurements, particularly triglycerides. However, many modern cholesterol tests can be performed without fasting. The pharmacist or trained staff will explain the procedure and ensure that the patient is comfortable and ready for the test.
2. **Sample Collection**: A small blood sample is collected from the patient, usually by pricking the fingertip with a lancet. The blood is then placed on a test strip or into a small vial, which is inserted into the lipid analyzer. This step is quick and minimally invasive, causing only a brief moment of discomfort for the patient.
3. **Measuring Cholesterol Levels**: The lipid analyzer processes the blood sample and provides readings for the patient's lipid profile, typically within a few minutes. The results include:

- **Total Cholesterol**: This is the sum of all cholesterol in the blood and is an important marker of overall cardiovascular health. Normal levels are typically below 200 mg/dL.
- **LDL Cholesterol**: Often referred to as "bad" cholesterol, high levels of LDL can lead to plaque buildup in the arteries, increasing the risk of heart disease. A desirable LDL level is less than 100 mg/dL.
- **HDL Cholesterol**: Known as "good" cholesterol, HDL helps remove excess cholesterol from the blood, reducing the risk of heart disease. Higher levels of HDL are considered protective, with levels of 60 mg/dL or higher being optimal.
- **Triglycerides**: These are a type of fat in the blood, and high levels can contribute to the hardening and narrowing of arteries. Normal levels are typically below 150 mg/dL.

4. **Interpreting the Results**: The pharmacist will interpret the cholesterol test results and discuss them with the patient. Depending on the readings, the pharmacist may provide advice on lifestyle changes, such as diet and exercise, to help improve or maintain healthy cholesterol levels. For example, if a patient has high LDL cholesterol, the pharmacist might recommend reducing saturated fat intake, increasing physical activity, and considering the use of cholesterol-lowering medications if necessary.
5. **Counseling and Referral**: If the cholesterol levels are outside the normal range, the pharmacist will counsel the patient on the importance of managing their lipid levels to reduce the risk of cardiovascular disease. The pharmacist may also refer the patient to their primary care physician for further evaluation and potential treatment. For instance, a patient with significantly elevated total cholesterol and LDL levels may need to undergo additional tests and possibly start on medication like statins to lower their cholesterol.

Importance of Cholesterol Testing in Community Pharmacy

Cholesterol testing in community pharmacies is essential for the early detection of dyslipidemia, a condition characterized by abnormal levels of cholesterol and other lipids in the blood. Early detection through regular screening allows patients to take proactive steps to manage their cholesterol levels and reduce their risk of heart disease and stroke.

For example, a patient who discovers during a routine pharmacy screening that they have high cholesterol can begin making lifestyle changes or start medication to lower their cholesterol before they experience any cardiovascular events. This proactive approach can prevent the progression of heart disease and improve long-term health outcomes.

Cholesterol testing in pharmacies also improves **access to care**, particularly for individuals who may not have regular contact with the healthcare system. Many people visit pharmacies more frequently than they visit doctors, making pharmacies an ideal location for preventive health screenings. By offering cholesterol testing, community pharmacies can reach a broader population, especially those at risk of cardiovascular diseases who might not seek regular medical check-ups.

In addition, cholesterol testing provides an opportunity for **patient education**. Pharmacists can educate patients about the importance of maintaining healthy cholesterol levels and the impact of diet, exercise, and other lifestyle factors on cardiovascular health. For instance, a pharmacist might explain how a diet high in fruits, vegetables, whole grains, and lean proteins can help lower LDL cholesterol and raise HDL cholesterol.

Moreover, regular cholesterol testing allows for **ongoing monitoring** of patients with known dyslipidemia or those at high risk of cardiovascular disease. Patients can have their cholesterol levels checked periodically at the pharmacy, enabling adjustments to their treatment plan as needed. This regular monitoring helps ensure that patients are effectively managing their cholesterol levels and reducing their risk of heart disease.

NINE

OTC MEDICATION AND COUNSELLING

9.1 Definition of OTC Medication

Over-the-counter (OTC) medications are pharmaceutical products that can be purchased by consumers directly from pharmacies, retail stores, or online platforms without the need for a prescription from a healthcare provider. These medications are used to treat common, self-limiting conditions such as headaches, colds, allergies, indigestion, minor pain, and other everyday health issues. OTC medications are considered safe and effective for use by the general public when taken according to the instructions provided on the label.

OTC medications encompass a wide range of drug categories, including analgesics, antipyretics, antacids, antihistamines, decongestants, cough suppressants, laxatives, and topical treatments, among others. For example, common OTC analgesics include paracetamol (acetaminophen) and ibuprofen, which are used to relieve pain and reduce fever. Antihistamines like cetirizine and loratadine are commonly used to manage symptoms of allergies, such as sneezing and itching.

The availability of OTC medications is governed by regulatory bodies, such as the Food and Drug Administration (FDA) in the United States or the Central Drugs Standard Control Organization (CDSCO) in India. These regulatory agencies evaluate the safety, efficacy, and labeling of OTC drugs before they can be sold to the public. They ensure that the benefits of the medication outweigh the risks when used as directed, and that the product labeling provides clear instructions and warnings to guide safe use.

OTC medications are designed for **self-care**, meaning that consumers can independently choose and use these products without professional supervision. This accessibility offers several advantages, including convenience, cost savings, and the ability to manage minor health conditions promptly. For instance, a person experiencing mild cold symptoms can easily purchase and use an OTC cold remedy, such as a combination of a decongestant and an antihistamine, without the need for a doctor's visit.

However, while OTC medications are generally safe when used appropriately, there is still potential for misuse, overuse, or interaction with other medications. For example, excessive use of OTC pain relievers like ibuprofen can lead to gastrointestinal issues or kidney damage, especially in individuals with pre-existing health conditions. Additionally, some OTC medications can interact with prescription drugs, leading to adverse effects or reduced efficacy of treatment. For instance, taking an antacid containing magnesium hydroxide alongside certain antibiotics can reduce the absorption and effectiveness of the antibiotic.

Therefore, it is crucial for consumers to carefully read and follow the instructions on the medication label, pay attention to dosage recommendations, and be aware of any warnings or contraindications. Pharmacists play a vital role in guiding consumers in the safe and effective use of OTC medications, offering advice on product selection, dosing, potential side effects, and interactions with other medications or health conditions. For example, a pharmacist might advise a patient with hypertension to avoid OTC decongestants that can raise blood pressure, suggesting an alternative product instead.

9.2.1 Pain Relievers

Pain relievers are among the most commonly used over-the-counter (OTC) medications, offering quick and accessible relief from various types of pain, including headaches, muscle aches, menstrual cramps, dental pain, and minor arthritis. These medications are widely available and play a significant role in managing mild to moderate pain without the need for a prescription. The two primary categories of OTC pain relievers are nonsteroidal anti-inflammatory drugs (NSAIDs) and acetaminophen (paracetamol).

NSAIDs (Nonsteroidal Anti-Inflammatory Drugs)

NSAIDs are a class of drugs that provide pain relief by reducing inflammation, which is often the underlying cause of pain. Common OTC

NSAIDs include ibuprofen, aspirin, and naproxen. These medications work by inhibiting the production of prostaglandins, substances in the body that promote inflammation, pain, and fever.

- **Ibuprofen**: Sold under brand names such as Advil and Brufen, ibuprofen is widely used for pain relief, fever reduction, and inflammation control. It is commonly recommended for conditions like headaches, menstrual cramps, and muscle aches. Ibuprofen is generally well-tolerated when used at the recommended doses, but it can cause gastrointestinal irritation, especially with long-term use. For example, taking ibuprofen on an empty stomach can increase the risk of stomach ulcers or bleeding.
- **Aspirin**: Aspirin, known by the brand name Bayer among others, is another popular NSAID that is used not only for pain relief but also for its antiplatelet effects, which help reduce the risk of heart attacks and strokes in certain populations. However, aspirin is not recommended for children due to the risk of Reye's syndrome, a rare but serious condition. In adults, aspirin should be used cautiously, especially in those with a history of gastrointestinal bleeding or those taking other blood-thinning medications.
- **Naproxen**: Available under brand names like Aleve, naproxen is an NSAID that is effective for longer-lasting pain relief compared to ibuprofen. It is often used for conditions such as arthritis, muscle pain, and menstrual cramps. Like other NSAIDs, naproxen can cause gastrointestinal side effects, and it should be used with caution in individuals with cardiovascular risk factors.

Acetaminophen (Paracetamol)

Acetaminophen, also known as paracetamol and sold under brand names like Tylenol and Panadol, is another widely used OTC pain reliever. Unlike NSAIDs, acetaminophen does not have anti-inflammatory properties, but it is effective in relieving pain and reducing fever. Acetaminophen works by inhibiting the production of prostaglandins in the brain, which helps to alleviate pain and fever.

Acetaminophen is generally considered safer than NSAIDs for individuals who have gastrointestinal issues, as it does not cause stomach irritation or increase the risk of bleeding. However, it is important to use acetaminophen within the recommended dosage limits, as excessive use can lead to severe liver damage. For example, taking more than 4,000 milligrams of acetaminophen in a day can result in acute liver failure, a potentially life-threatening condition. Patients with pre-existing liver conditions or those who consume alcohol regularly should use acetaminophen with caution and consult a healthcare provider if necessary.

Counseling Considerations for Pain Relievers

Pharmacists play a crucial role in advising patients on the appropriate use of OTC pain relievers. When counseling patients, pharmacists should consider the following factors:

- **Appropriate Selection**: Pharmacists should help patients choose the most suitable pain reliever based on their specific needs, medical history, and potential risk factors. For example, ibuprofen may be recommended for a patient with menstrual cramps, while acetaminophen might be a better option for someone with a history of stomach ulcers.
- **Dosage and Duration**: Patients should be advised on the correct dosage and the maximum duration of use for OTC pain relievers. For instance, ibuprofen should not be taken for more than 10 days for pain relief unless directed by a doctor, and acetaminophen should not exceed the daily recommended dose to avoid liver damage.
- **Potential Interactions**: Pharmacists should review the patient's medication history to identify any potential drug interactions. For example, patients taking blood thinners like warfarin should be cautious when using NSAIDs due to the increased risk of bleeding.
- **Side Effects and Precautions**: Patients should be informed about the potential side effects of pain relievers, such as gastrointestinal irritation with NSAIDs or liver toxicity with acetaminophen. Pharmacists should also advise patients on when to seek medical attention if they experience any severe or unusual symptoms.

9.2.2 Cold and Flu Medications

Cold and flu medications are among the most frequently used over-the-counter (OTC) products, providing relief from the common symptoms associated with viral respiratory infections. These symptoms can include cough, congestion, runny nose, sore throat, headache, fever, and body aches. Cold and flu medications are typically available in various formulations, such as tablets, capsules, syrups, lozenges, and nasal sprays, allowing consumers to choose the form that best suits their needs.

Types of Cold and Flu Medications

Cold and flu medications generally contain one or more active ingredients designed to target specific symptoms. Some of the most common categories of these medications include:

- **Decongestants**: Decongestants help reduce nasal congestion by narrowing the blood vessels in the nasal passages, thereby decreasing swelling and mucus production. The most common OTC decongestants are pseudoephedrine and phenylephrine. Pseudoephedrine is available behind the pharmacy counter in many countries due to its potential misuse in the production of methamphetamine, while phenylephrine is available on the shelves. For example, pseudoephedrine is found in products like Sudafed, and phenylephrine is in products like Sudafed PE. Decongestants can cause side effects such as increased blood pressure, insomnia, and nervousness, so they should be used with caution, especially in individuals with hypertension or heart conditions.
- **Antihistamines**: Antihistamines are often included in cold and flu medications to alleviate symptoms like a runny nose, sneezing, and watery eyes, which are caused by the body's release of histamine in response to the virus. First-generation antihistamines, such as diphenhydramine (found in Benadryl), are effective but can cause drowsiness. Second-generation antihistamines, like loratadine and cetirizine, are less sedating and are also used to treat allergy symptoms. However, for cold and flu relief, first-generation antihistamines are more commonly included due to their added benefit of inducing sleep, which can be helpful when dealing with nighttime symptoms.
- **Cough Suppressants and Expectorants**: Cough suppressants, or antitussives, such as dextromethorphan, are used to reduce the frequency and intensity of coughing, making them particularly useful for dry, non-productive coughs. Dextromethorphan is commonly found in products like Robitussin DM and Delsym. Expectorants, on the other hand, such as guaifenesin, help thin and loosen mucus in the airways, making it easier to cough up and clear congestion. Guaifenesin is found in products like Mucinex. These medications can be particularly beneficial for productive coughs where mucus is present.
- **Analgesics and Antipyretics**: Analgesics such as acetaminophen and ibuprofen are included in many cold and flu formulations to relieve pain, such as headaches, sore throat, and muscle aches, as well as to reduce fever. These medications help manage the general discomfort associated

with colds and the flu, making it easier for patients to rest and recover. For example, products like DayQuil and NyQuil contain acetaminophen for pain relief and fever reduction.

- **Combination Products**: Many cold and flu medications are combination products that contain multiple active ingredients to address several symptoms simultaneously. For example, a typical multi-symptom cold medicine might contain a decongestant, an antihistamine, an analgesic, and a cough suppressant. These products offer convenience by allowing patients to treat multiple symptoms with a single medication. However, it is important for consumers to be aware of the active ingredients to avoid duplicating therapy, especially when taking other medications. For instance, a patient taking a separate analgesic should avoid a cold medicine that also contains acetaminophen to prevent accidental overdose.

Counseling Considerations for Cold and Flu Medications

When advising patients on the use of OTC cold and flu medications, pharmacists should consider several important factors:

- **Symptom Matching**: Pharmacists should help patients choose the most appropriate medication based on their specific symptoms. For example, a patient with nasal congestion and a dry cough may benefit from a combination of a decongestant and a cough suppressant, while a patient with a runny nose and sneezing may require an antihistamine.
- **Potential Interactions**: Pharmacists should review the patient's medication history to identify any potential interactions between cold and flu medications and other drugs the patient may be taking. For example, patients on monoamine oxidase inhibitors (MAOIs) should avoid decongestants like pseudoephedrine and phenylephrine due to the risk of severe hypertensive reactions.
- **Side Effects and Precautions**: Patients should be informed about the potential side effects of cold and flu medications. For example, decongestants can cause elevated blood pressure and insomnia, while first-generation antihistamines can cause drowsiness and dry mouth. Pharmacists should also advise patients on when to seek medical attention if they experience severe or unusual symptoms, such as difficulty breathing or chest pain.

- **Duration of Use**: Patients should be counseled on the appropriate duration of use for cold and flu medications. Most OTC products are intended for short-term use, typically no more than 7 to 10 days. If symptoms persist beyond this period, the patient should be advised to consult a healthcare provider, as prolonged symptoms may indicate a more serious condition that requires medical evaluation.
- **Non-Pharmacological Recommendations**: In addition to recommending OTC medications, pharmacists can also suggest non-pharmacological measures to alleviate cold and flu symptoms. These might include staying hydrated, using a humidifier to ease congestion, getting plenty of rest, and consuming warm liquids like herbal teas or broths to soothe a sore throat.

9.3.1 Appropriate Use

Counseling on the appropriate use of over-the-counter (OTC) medications is a critical responsibility of pharmacists, ensuring that patients use these accessible treatments safely and effectively. While OTC medications are generally safe for self-treatment of minor health issues, their misuse can lead to adverse effects, drug interactions, and other health risks. Therefore, it is essential for pharmacists to educate patients on how to use these medications correctly, guiding them through proper selection, dosing, and understanding of potential risks.

Selection of OTC Medications

The first step in ensuring the appropriate use of OTC medications is helping patients select the right product for their specific symptoms and conditions. Pharmacists should ask patients about their symptoms, medical history, and any other medications they are currently taking. For example, if a patient is experiencing mild joint pain and has a history of gastric ulcers, the pharmacist might recommend acetaminophen instead of an NSAID like ibuprofen, which could exacerbate their stomach issues.

It is also important to consider the patient's age, existing health conditions, and any known allergies. For instance, elderly patients may be more sensitive to the sedative effects of certain antihistamines or may have kidney function issues that require lower doses of medications. Similarly, patients with chronic conditions like hypertension or diabetes may need to avoid certain decongestants or other OTC products that could interfere with their primary treatment.

Correct Dosing and Administration

One of the most common issues with OTC medication use is incorrect dosing, which can lead to ineffective treatment or, conversely, overdose and toxicity. Pharmacists should educate patients on the importance of following the dosing instructions on the medication label or as directed by a healthcare provider. This includes understanding the recommended dose, the frequency of administration, and the maximum allowable dose within a 24-hour period.

For example, acetaminophen, though generally safe when used correctly, can cause severe liver damage if taken in excessive amounts. Patients should be advised not to exceed 4,000 mg per day and to be cautious when using multiple products that may contain acetaminophen, such as combination cold and flu medications. Similarly, ibuprofen and other NSAIDs should be taken with food to minimize gastrointestinal side effects, and patients should be warned not to exceed the recommended duration of use without consulting a doctor.

Understanding Potential Risks

While OTC medications are readily available, they are not without risks. Pharmacists play a crucial role in informing patients about the potential side effects, drug interactions, and contraindications associated with OTC products. For instance, patients using antihistamines for allergies or cold symptoms should be made aware of the potential for drowsiness, which could impair their ability to drive or operate machinery. Additionally, patients with certain chronic conditions, such as cardiovascular disease or asthma, may need to avoid specific OTC medications that could worsen their condition.

Pharmacists should also educate patients about the signs of serious side effects or allergic reactions, advising them to seek immediate medical attention if they experience symptoms like difficulty breathing, swelling, or severe skin reactions. Moreover, patients should be reminded to check the expiration dates on OTC medications and to store them properly to ensure their effectiveness and safety.

Avoiding Drug Interactions

Another critical aspect of counseling on appropriate OTC medication use is preventing potential drug interactions. Many OTC products can interact with prescription medications, dietary supplements, or other OTC drugs, leading to reduced efficacy or increased risk of adverse effects. Pharmacists should ask patients about all the medications and supplements they are taking to identify any potential interactions.

For example, patients taking blood thinners like warfarin should avoid NSAIDs such as ibuprofen and aspirin, as these can increase the risk of bleeding. Similarly, patients on certain antidepressants or antipsychotics should be cautious with decongestants like pseudoephedrine, which can raise blood pressure and cause other cardiovascular issues.

Monitoring and Follow-Up

Pharmacists should encourage patients to monitor their symptoms and the effectiveness of the OTC medication. If symptoms persist or worsen after a few days of treatment, or if the patient experiences any adverse effects, they should be advised to seek further medical evaluation. Additionally, pharmacists can offer to follow up with the patient to ensure that the medication is working as expected and that there are no issues with adherence or side effects.

9.3.2 Potential Risks and Side Effects

While over-the-counter (OTC) medications are generally considered safe for treating minor ailments, they are not without potential risks and side effects. Understanding these risks is crucial for both patients and healthcare providers to ensure the safe and effective use of these medications. Pharmacists play a key role in educating patients about the potential adverse effects and helping them to make informed decisions about their medication use.

Common Side Effects of OTC Medications

Most OTC medications have side effects, which can range from mild to severe. Common side effects often depend on the specific medication and the condition being treated. For example:

- **NSAIDs (Nonsteroidal Anti-Inflammatory Drugs)** such as ibuprofen and aspirin are widely used for pain relief and inflammation reduction. However, they can cause gastrointestinal irritation, leading to symptoms like stomach pain, nausea, heartburn, and even ulcers or gastrointestinal bleeding with prolonged use. NSAIDs can also increase the risk of cardiovascular events, such as heart attack and stroke, particularly in patients with pre-existing heart conditions.
- **Antihistamines**, commonly used for allergies and cold symptoms, can cause drowsiness, dry mouth, and blurred vision. First-generation antihistamines like diphenhydramine are particularly known for their sedative effects, which can impair a patient's ability to perform tasks that require alertness, such as driving. On the other hand, second-generation

antihistamines, like loratadine, are less sedating but can still cause side effects in some individuals.

- **Decongestants** like pseudoephedrine and phenylephrine are effective in relieving nasal congestion but can lead to increased blood pressure, palpitations, and nervousness. These side effects make decongestants unsuitable for patients with hypertension or heart disease. Prolonged use of decongestant nasal sprays can also lead to rebound congestion, where the nasal passages become more congested once the medication is discontinued.
- **Cough suppressants and expectorants** have their own sets of side effects. For instance, dextromethorphan, a common cough suppressant, can cause dizziness, drowsiness, and, in higher doses, may lead to hallucinations or abuse. Guaifenesin, an expectorant, is generally well-tolerated but can cause gastrointestinal discomfort, including nausea and vomiting.
- **Acetaminophen (Paracetamol)** is a commonly used analgesic and antipyretic. While generally safe at recommended doses, excessive intake of acetaminophen can cause severe liver damage. This risk is particularly high when patients inadvertently take multiple acetaminophen-containing products, leading to cumulative doses that exceed the safe limit. Symptoms of liver toxicity might not appear immediately, making it important for patients to be aware of the risks of overdose.

Risks of Drug Interactions

OTC medications can interact with prescription drugs, other OTC products, and dietary supplements, leading to potentially harmful effects. For example:

- **NSAIDs** can interact with anticoagulants (blood thinners) such as warfarin, increasing the risk of bleeding. They can also reduce the effectiveness of antihypertensive medications, making blood pressure harder to control.
- **Decongestants** like pseudoephedrine can interact with monoamine oxidase inhibitors (MAOIs), a class of antidepressants, leading to dangerously high blood pressure.
- **Antacids** and **H2 blockers** (e.g., ranitidine) used for heartburn relief can interfere with the absorption of other medications, such as certain antibiotics and antifungals, reducing their effectiveness.

- **Herbal supplements** such as St. John's Wort can interact with a variety of OTC and prescription medications, leading to reduced drug effectiveness or increased risk of side effects. For example, St. John's Wort can reduce the effectiveness of oral contraceptives and increase the risk of serotonin syndrome when taken with antidepressants.

Long-Term Use and Misuse of OTC Medications

While OTC medications are intended for short-term use, many patients may use them for extended periods, leading to potential health risks. For example, long-term use of **laxatives** can lead to dependency, where the bowel becomes reliant on the medication to function properly. Similarly, overuse of **nasal decongestant sprays** can lead to rebound congestion, worsening the condition the medication was meant to treat.

Misuse of OTC medications is another significant risk. Patients may assume that because these medications are available without a prescription, they are completely safe and may take higher doses than recommended or use them for unapproved purposes. For instance, dextromethorphan, when taken in large quantities, can produce psychoactive effects, leading to abuse, especially among teenagers.

Counseling on Potential Risks and Side Effects

Pharmacists play a crucial role in counseling patients about the potential risks and side effects of OTC medications. This involves:

- **Educating patients** about the correct use of OTC medications, including the importance of adhering to recommended doses and duration of use. Pharmacists should emphasize that "more is not better" and that exceeding the recommended dose can lead to serious health risks.
- **Reviewing the patient's medication history** to identify potential drug interactions. Pharmacists should ask patients about all the medications and supplements they are taking, including herbal products, to prevent harmful interactions.
- **Warning patients about specific risks** associated with long-term use of certain OTC medications. For instance, pharmacists should advise patients against the prolonged use of NSAIDs without medical supervision, especially if they have a history of gastrointestinal issues or cardiovascular disease.
- **Encouraging patients to seek medical advice** if their symptoms persist or worsen despite OTC treatment. This ensures that underlying

conditions are properly diagnosed and treated, rather than being masked by OTC medications.

TEN

HEALTH EDUCATION AND PROMOTION

10.1 WHO Definition of Health

The World Health Organization (WHO) defines health not merely as the absence of disease or infirmity but as a state of complete physical, mental, and social well-being. This comprehensive definition, established in 1948, emphasizes that health is a multifaceted concept that extends beyond the simple notion of being free from illness. It acknowledges the importance of various dimensions of health, including physical fitness, mental stability, and the ability to engage in fulfilling social interactions and relationships.

Physical well-being refers to the optimal functioning of the body and its systems. It encompasses maintaining a healthy lifestyle through balanced nutrition, regular physical activity, adequate rest, and avoidance of harmful behaviors such as smoking and excessive alcohol consumption. For example, a person who maintains a healthy weight, exercises regularly, and eats a balanced diet is more likely to have a strong immune system, lower risk of chronic diseases, and overall better physical health.

Mental well-being involves emotional stability, psychological resilience, and the ability to cope with stress, anxiety, and other mental challenges. It includes factors such as self-esteem, cognitive functioning, and the capacity to enjoy life and maintain a sense of purpose. For instance, a person with good mental health is able to manage daily stressors effectively, maintain positive relationships, and adapt to changes and challenges in life. Mental health is as important as physical health, and both are deeply interconnected.

Social well-being reflects the quality of an individual's relationships with others and their ability to contribute to the community. It includes having supportive networks of family, friends, and colleagues, as well as the ability to communicate, empathize, and cooperate with others. Social well-being also encompasses an individual's role in society and their ability to participate in community activities and contribute to social cohesion. For example, strong social connections and community involvement are associated with lower rates of mental health issues and increased longevity.

The WHO's definition of health also implies a **holistic approach** to health promotion and disease prevention. It encourages healthcare providers, policymakers, and individuals to consider all aspects of health when developing strategies for improving population health. This means addressing not only physical ailments but also the social determinants of health, such as education, income, housing, and access to healthcare services. For example, public health initiatives aimed at reducing obesity must consider factors like access to healthy food, opportunities for physical activity, and education about nutrition.

In the context of **health education and promotion**, the WHO's definition of health serves as a foundation for developing comprehensive programs that address the diverse needs of individuals and communities. Health education involves providing people with the knowledge and skills they need to make informed decisions about their health, while health promotion focuses on creating environments that support healthy behaviors. For instance, a health promotion campaign might include initiatives to improve access to nutritious food in underserved areas, along with education about healthy eating habits.

The WHO's definition also highlights the importance of **preventive care** and the need for healthcare systems to focus on maintaining health rather than just treating illness. Preventive care includes regular health screenings, vaccinations, and lifestyle interventions that reduce the risk of developing chronic diseases. For example, regular blood pressure checks and cholesterol screenings can help detect early signs of cardiovascular disease, allowing for timely intervention and reducing the likelihood of serious health complications.

10.2.2 Care for Pregnant and Breastfeeding Women

Care for pregnant and breastfeeding women is a critical aspect of health education and promotion, as the well-being of both the mother and child is highly dependent on the quality of care provided during these stages.

Pregnancy and breastfeeding are times of significant physiological and emotional changes, and adequate care is essential to ensure positive outcomes for both the mother and the baby. This care involves not only medical attention but also education, nutritional support, mental health care, and social support.

Nutritional Support

Proper nutrition is vital during pregnancy and breastfeeding, as it directly affects the health and development of the baby as well as the mother's well-being. During pregnancy, women need to consume a balanced diet rich in essential nutrients such as folic acid, iron, calcium, and protein. Folic acid is particularly important in the early stages of pregnancy to prevent neural tube defects in the developing fetus. Iron is crucial for preventing anemia, which is common during pregnancy due to increased blood volume. For example, pregnant women are often advised to take prenatal vitamins that include these key nutrients to support their nutritional needs.

Breastfeeding women also require a nutrient-dense diet to produce sufficient and high-quality breast milk for their infants. This includes a higher intake of calories, protein, and fluids. For instance, a breastfeeding mother might need to consume an additional 500 calories per day compared to her pre-pregnancy intake. Proper hydration is equally important, as dehydration can affect milk production. Health education for pregnant and breastfeeding women should emphasize the importance of maintaining a healthy diet and provide guidance on how to achieve nutritional balance.

Prenatal and Postnatal Care

Regular prenatal check-ups are essential for monitoring the health of both the mother and the baby throughout pregnancy. These check-ups allow healthcare providers to track the baby's growth, screen for potential complications, and provide necessary vaccinations and supplements. For example, prenatal visits typically include ultrasounds, blood pressure monitoring, and tests for gestational diabetes. Early detection of issues such as preeclampsia or gestational diabetes allows for timely interventions that can prevent serious health problems.

Postnatal care is equally important, focusing on the mother's recovery after childbirth and the newborn's health. Postnatal visits usually include physical exams, mental health screenings, and guidance on breastfeeding and infant care. For instance, healthcare providers might check for postpartum depression and provide support or referrals if needed.

Education on topics such as breastfeeding techniques, newborn care, and contraception is also a critical component of postnatal care.

Mental Health Support

Pregnancy and the postpartum period can be challenging times for women's mental health. Hormonal changes, physical discomfort, and the stress of preparing for a new baby can lead to mental health issues such as anxiety and depression. Postpartum depression, in particular, is a serious condition that affects many new mothers and can have a profound impact on their ability to care for their baby.

Health education and promotion should include awareness about the signs and symptoms of prenatal and postpartum depression, as well as available resources for support. For example, women should be informed about the importance of seeking help if they experience persistent feelings of sadness, hopelessness, or difficulty bonding with their baby. Mental health support can include counseling, support groups, and, when necessary, medication under the guidance of a healthcare provider.

Breastfeeding Education and Support

Breastfeeding offers numerous health benefits for both the mother and the baby, including protection against infections, reduced risk of chronic diseases, and bonding between mother and child. However, breastfeeding can also present challenges, particularly for first-time mothers. Common issues include difficulties with latching, concerns about milk supply, and physical discomfort.

Health education programs should provide comprehensive breastfeeding education, including information on the benefits of breastfeeding, proper breastfeeding techniques, and how to address common challenges. Lactation consultants can offer valuable support, helping mothers to establish and maintain breastfeeding, especially in the early days after birth. For instance, a lactation consultant might assist a new mother in finding a comfortable breastfeeding position or suggest methods to increase milk production.

Social Support and Community Resources

Social support plays a crucial role in the health and well-being of pregnant and breastfeeding women. Support from family, friends, and the community can reduce stress, improve mental health, and promote better outcomes for both mother and baby. Community resources, such as support groups for new mothers, can provide a space for women to share their experiences, receive encouragement, and learn from others.

Health promotion efforts should include information about available community resources, such as prenatal classes, breastfeeding support groups, and parenting workshops. These resources can help women feel more confident and supported throughout their pregnancy and breastfeeding journey. For example, attending a prenatal class might help a woman feel more prepared for childbirth, while joining a breastfeeding support group can provide ongoing encouragement and practical advice.

10.2.3 Geriatric Patient Care

Geriatric patient care is a crucial aspect of health education and promotion, focusing on the unique needs and challenges faced by the elderly population. As people age, they often experience a range of physical, cognitive, and social changes that require specialized care and attention. Effective geriatric care involves not only addressing the medical conditions common in older adults but also promoting overall well-being, independence, and quality of life.

Physical Health Management

As individuals age, they are more likely to develop chronic health conditions such as hypertension, diabetes, arthritis, and heart disease. Managing these conditions requires a comprehensive approach that includes regular medical check-ups, appropriate medication management, and lifestyle modifications. For example, older adults with diabetes need to monitor their blood glucose levels regularly, adhere to a diabetic diet, and engage in regular physical activity to manage their condition effectively.

Medication management is a particularly important aspect of geriatric care, as older adults are often prescribed multiple medications for various conditions. Polypharmacy, or the use of multiple medications, increases the risk of adverse drug interactions, side effects, and medication non-adherence. Pharmacists and healthcare providers play a key role in reviewing and optimizing medication regimens for geriatric patients, ensuring that they are taking the correct medications at the right doses and times. For instance, simplifying a medication regimen by using combination pills or providing clear instructions can help reduce the risk of medication errors.

Cognitive Health and Mental Well-being

Cognitive decline is a common concern among the elderly, with conditions such as dementia and Alzheimer's disease affecting a significant portion of the aging population. Early detection and intervention are essential in managing cognitive decline and slowing its progression.

Geriatric care should include regular cognitive assessments to monitor memory, reasoning, and problem-solving abilities. If cognitive decline is detected, healthcare providers can implement strategies to support mental functioning, such as cognitive therapy, memory exercises, and, when appropriate, medications.

Mental health is another critical component of geriatric care. Depression, anxiety, and loneliness are prevalent among older adults, often due to factors such as social isolation, loss of loved ones, and physical limitations. Mental health support for geriatric patients should include counseling, social engagement opportunities, and, when needed, medication to manage symptoms. For example, participation in community activities or support groups can help reduce feelings of loneliness and improve overall mental well-being.

Nutritional Support

Nutrition plays a vital role in maintaining health and preventing disease in older adults. However, many geriatric patients face challenges related to nutrition, such as decreased appetite, difficulty chewing or swallowing, and limited access to healthy foods. Malnutrition can lead to weakened immunity, muscle loss, and an increased risk of falls and fractures.

Healthcare providers should educate geriatric patients and their caregivers about the importance of a balanced diet rich in essential nutrients like protein, calcium, vitamin D, and fiber. For example, older adults may benefit from smaller, more frequent meals that are easier to eat and digest, as well as supplements to address specific nutrient deficiencies. Additionally, hydration is crucial for elderly patients, as dehydration can exacerbate health issues like urinary tract infections and kidney problems.

Mobility and Fall Prevention

Mobility is a significant concern for many older adults, as reduced strength, balance, and coordination increase the risk of falls and related injuries. Fall prevention is a key focus of geriatric care, involving both environmental modifications and physical interventions. For instance, installing grab bars in bathrooms, improving lighting, and removing tripping hazards in the home can significantly reduce the risk of falls.

Physical therapy and regular exercise are also important for maintaining mobility and preventing falls. Exercises that focus on strength, flexibility, and balance can help older adults stay active and independent. For example, tai chi and gentle yoga are popular activities that improve balance and coordination while being accessible to individuals with varying levels of physical ability.

Social Support and Engagement

Social support is essential for the overall well-being of geriatric patients. Social isolation and loneliness can lead to depression, cognitive decline, and a lower quality of life. Encouraging older adults to engage in social activities, whether through community centers, senior clubs, or online platforms, can help them stay connected and maintain a sense of purpose.

Caregivers and family members play a vital role in providing social support and should be included in the care plan for geriatric patients. Educating caregivers on the importance of regular interaction, emotional support, and respite care can help them better manage the challenges of caregiving while ensuring the elderly receive the attention and care they need.

End-of-Life Care and Advanced Care Planning

End-of-life care is a sensitive but important aspect of geriatric care. It involves discussing and planning for the patient's preferences regarding medical interventions, palliative care, and hospice services. Advanced care planning allows elderly patients to make informed decisions about their care and ensures that their wishes are respected when they are no longer able to communicate them.

Healthcare providers should facilitate open and compassionate conversations with geriatric patients and their families about end-of-life care options, including pain management, comfort care, and the use of life-sustaining treatments. For example, discussing the benefits of palliative care in managing symptoms and improving quality of life can help patients and their families make decisions that align with their values and goals.

10.3.1 Tuberculosis

Tuberculosis (TB) is one of the most prevalent communicable diseases worldwide, particularly in developing countries. It is caused by the bacterium *Mycobacterium tuberculosis*, which primarily affects the lungs but can also spread to other parts of the body, such as the kidneys, spine, and brain. TB is transmitted through airborne droplets when an infected person coughs, sneezes, or speaks, making it a highly contagious disease. Despite being curable and preventable, TB remains a significant public health challenge, particularly in regions with high rates of poverty, malnutrition, and HIV co-infection.

Prevention of Tuberculosis

Preventing TB requires a multi-faceted approach, including vaccination, early detection, infection control, and public health education. The Bacille Calmette-Guérin (BCG) vaccine is widely used in many countries as a preventive measure against TB, particularly in infants and young children. While the BCG vaccine does not provide complete protection against all forms of TB, it is effective in preventing severe forms of the disease, such as TB meningitis and miliary TB in children.

Early detection and treatment of active TB cases are crucial in preventing the spread of the disease. Screening programs, particularly in high-risk populations such as healthcare workers, people living with HIV, and individuals in close contact with TB patients, are essential in identifying cases early. For example, the use of tuberculin skin tests (TST) or interferon-gamma release assays (IGRAs) helps in detecting latent TB infections, which can be treated to prevent progression to active TB.

Infection control measures in healthcare settings and communities are vital in preventing the transmission of TB. These include the use of personal protective equipment (PPE), such as N95 respirators, implementing proper ventilation in crowded spaces, and ensuring that patients with active TB are isolated until they are no longer infectious. Public health education plays a critical role in raising awareness about TB transmission, symptoms, and the importance of completing the full course of treatment to prevent drug-resistant TB.

Management of Tuberculosis

The management of TB involves a structured treatment regimen, primarily using a combination of antibiotics over an extended period. The standard treatment for drug-sensitive TB includes a six-month regimen of four first-line drugs: isoniazid, rifampicin, pyrazinamide, and ethambutol. This initial intensive phase, typically lasting two months, is followed by a continuation phase with isoniazid and rifampicin for four more months. Adherence to the full treatment regimen is critical to ensure the complete eradication of the bacteria and to prevent the development of drug-resistant TB strains.

One of the major challenges in TB management is the emergence of multidrug-resistant TB (MDR-TB) and extensively drug-resistant TB (XDR-TB), which are resistant to first-line and some second-line drugs, respectively. Treating these forms of TB requires the use of more toxic and less effective second-line drugs, often over a longer duration. The treatment for MDR-TB can last up to 20 months or more and includes drugs such as fluoroquinolones and injectable agents like amikacin or capreomycin.

Directly observed treatment, short-course (DOTS) is a key strategy recommended by the WHO to ensure that patients adhere to their treatment regimens. Under DOTS, healthcare workers or trained volunteers directly observe patients taking their medication, which helps improve adherence and treatment outcomes. For instance, a community health worker may visit a patient's home daily or several times a week to administer medication and monitor the patient's progress.

In addition to pharmacological treatment, the management of TB requires addressing the social determinants of health that contribute to the disease's spread and impact. This includes improving living conditions, reducing overcrowding, enhancing nutrition, and addressing co-infections such as HIV. For example, integrating TB and HIV services ensures that patients receive comprehensive care, as TB is the leading cause of death among people living with HIV.

Public Health Education and Promotion

Public health education is essential in controlling the spread of TB and ensuring that affected individuals seek timely diagnosis and treatment. Educational campaigns should focus on increasing awareness of TB symptoms, such as a persistent cough, fever, night sweats, and weight loss, as well as the importance of seeking medical attention if these symptoms persist. For instance, posters, radio broadcasts, and community outreach programs can be used to disseminate information about TB in high-risk areas.

Promoting adherence to TB treatment is another crucial aspect of public health education. Patients need to understand the importance of completing the full course of treatment, even if they start feeling better, to prevent the development of drug-resistant TB. Healthcare providers should emphasize that stopping treatment prematurely or missing doses can lead to treatment failure and increase the risk of spreading TB to others.

10.3.2 Hepatitis

Hepatitis refers to the inflammation of the liver, commonly caused by viral infections, though it can also result from alcohol consumption, toxins, medications, and autoimmune diseases. The most prevalent forms of viral hepatitis are hepatitis A, B, C, D, and E, each caused by different viruses with varying modes of transmission, clinical manifestations, and long-term outcomes. Hepatitis poses a significant public health challenge globally, particularly in low- and middle-income countries where access to preventive measures and treatment may be limited.

Prevention of Hepatitis

The prevention of hepatitis varies depending on the type of virus involved.

- **Hepatitis A and E**: These forms of hepatitis are primarily transmitted through the ingestion of contaminated food or water, making hygiene and sanitation critical in prevention efforts. Vaccination is available for hepatitis A and is highly effective in preventing the disease. For instance, travelers to regions with poor sanitation are often advised to receive the hepatitis A vaccine. Improving access to clean water, promoting good hand hygiene, and ensuring proper food safety practices are essential measures to prevent hepatitis A and E outbreaks.
- **Hepatitis B and C**: These viruses are transmitted through blood and bodily fluids, making prevention strategies focus on reducing the risk of exposure. Hepatitis B can be prevented through vaccination, which is included in the routine immunization schedule for infants in many countries. For example, the hepatitis B vaccine is typically administered in three doses, starting at birth. Hepatitis C, however, does not have a vaccine, so prevention efforts focus on minimizing risks associated with blood transfusions, unsafe injections, and needle sharing among drug users. Screening of blood products, safe injection practices, and harm reduction programs for people who inject drugs are critical components of hepatitis B and C prevention.
- **Hepatitis D**: This virus requires the presence of hepatitis B to replicate, so prevention is closely tied to controlling hepatitis B. Vaccination against hepatitis B also prevents hepatitis D, as the latter cannot exist without the former.

Public health education plays a crucial role in preventing hepatitis by raising awareness about the modes of transmission and the importance of vaccination and safe practices. For instance, educational campaigns can target high-risk populations, such as healthcare workers, individuals with multiple sexual partners, and people who inject drugs, to encourage behaviors that reduce the risk of hepatitis transmission.

Management of Hepatitis

The management of hepatitis depends on the type and severity of the infection.

- **Hepatitis A and E**: These forms of hepatitis are typically acute and self-limiting, meaning they do not usually lead to chronic liver disease. Management is primarily supportive, focusing on maintaining hydration, rest, and adequate nutrition. Most individuals recover fully without the need for antiviral treatment. However, in severe cases, particularly in pregnant women with hepatitis E, hospitalization may be required.
- **Hepatitis B and C**: Chronic hepatitis B and C infections can lead to serious complications, including cirrhosis, liver failure, and hepatocellular carcinoma (liver cancer). The management of chronic hepatitis B involves the use of antiviral medications such as tenofovir or entecavir, which help suppress the virus and prevent liver damage. For instance, patients with chronic hepatitis B may require long-term treatment to control the infection and reduce the risk of liver-related complications.

The management of chronic hepatitis C has been revolutionized by the development of direct-acting antivirals (DAAs), which offer high cure rates with shorter treatment durations and fewer side effects compared to older therapies. For example, a typical course of DAA therapy can cure hepatitis C in 8 to 12 weeks. Early detection and treatment are crucial in preventing the progression of liver disease in individuals with chronic hepatitis C.

- **Hepatitis D**: The management of hepatitis D is challenging, as there are limited treatment options available. Pegylated interferon is currently the primary treatment, but it has variable efficacy and significant side effects. Research into new treatments for hepatitis D is ongoing, with the goal of improving outcomes for affected individuals.

Public Health Education and Promotion

Public health education is vital in controlling the spread of hepatitis and ensuring that individuals at risk are aware of the importance of prevention, early detection, and treatment. Education campaigns should focus on promoting vaccination, particularly for hepatitis A and B, and encouraging safe practices such as the use of sterile needles and safe sexual behaviors to prevent hepatitis B and C.

For individuals with chronic hepatitis, education should emphasize the importance of regular monitoring and adherence to treatment to prevent liver disease progression. For instance, patients with chronic hepatitis B should be advised to undergo regular liver function tests and screenings for liver cancer, as early detection of complications can significantly improve outcomes.

10.3.3 Malaria

Malaria is a life-threatening disease caused by parasites of the *Plasmodium* species, which are transmitted to humans through the bites of infected female *Anopheles* mosquitoes. Malaria is endemic in many tropical and subtropical regions, particularly in Africa, South Asia, and parts of Latin America. Despite being preventable and treatable, malaria remains a major public health challenge, especially in areas with limited access to healthcare and preventive measures. Each year, malaria causes hundreds of thousands of deaths, particularly among young children and pregnant women.

Prevention of Malaria

Preventing malaria requires a combination of vector control, preventive medication, and public health education. **Vector control** is the primary method of reducing the transmission of malaria and involves reducing the population of *Anopheles* mosquitoes and limiting human exposure to mosquito bites. Two of the most effective vector control measures are the use of insecticide-treated bed nets (ITNs) and indoor residual spraying (IRS).

- **Insecticide-treated bed nets (ITNs)**: Sleeping under ITNs is one of the most effective ways to prevent mosquito bites, especially in areas where malaria transmission is highest. The insecticide on the nets kills or repels mosquitoes, reducing the risk of infection. In countries where malaria is endemic, distributing ITNs is a key public health intervention. For example, in sub-Saharan Africa, mass distribution campaigns have significantly reduced malaria transmission and mortality rates.
- **Indoor residual spraying (IRS)**: IRS involves spraying the interior walls of homes with insecticides to kill mosquitoes that rest on the surfaces after feeding. This intervention is particularly effective in areas with high malaria transmission and can provide protection for several months. IRS has been widely implemented in regions with seasonal malaria transmission, such as parts of India and Southern Africa.

Preventive medication, also known as chemoprophylaxis, is recommended for individuals traveling to areas where malaria is endemic, as well as for pregnant women and young children living in these regions.

Drugs like chloroquine, doxycycline, mefloquine, and atovaquone-proguanil are used to prevent malaria infection. For example, travelers to high-risk areas may be advised to begin taking prophylactic medication before their trip, continue taking it during their stay, and continue for a period after leaving the area to ensure full protection.

In addition to vector control and medication, **public health education** plays a vital role in preventing malaria. Educating communities about the importance of using bed nets, wearing protective clothing, and seeking treatment early when symptoms arise is essential for reducing the spread of malaria. Public health campaigns often focus on promoting awareness about the early signs of malaria, such as fever, chills, headache, and fatigue, so that individuals seek prompt medical care.

Management of Malaria

The management of malaria depends on the type of *Plasmodium* species causing the infection and the severity of the disease. The two most common forms of malaria are caused by *Plasmodium falciparum* and *Plasmodium vivax*, with *P. falciparum* being the most dangerous due to its potential to cause severe and life-threatening complications.

- **Uncomplicated malaria**: The treatment of uncomplicated malaria typically involves oral antimalarial drugs. The most commonly used treatment for *P. falciparum* malaria is artemisinin-based combination therapy (ACT). ACTs combine an artemisinin derivative with a partner drug to ensure the effective elimination of the parasite from the bloodstream. For example, artesunate combined with lumefantrine is one of the most widely used ACTs in areas with drug-resistant malaria. In regions where *P. vivax* is more common, primaquine is often added to the treatment regimen to target the liver stage of the parasite and prevent relapse.
- **Severe malaria**: Severe malaria is a medical emergency that requires immediate treatment with intravenous (IV) antimalarial drugs. Artesunate is the preferred treatment for severe malaria due to its rapid action in reducing the parasite load. Patients with severe malaria often require supportive care, including IV fluids, blood transfusions, and respiratory support, depending on the complications they experience. For instance, cerebral malaria, a severe form of the disease affecting the brain, can lead to coma and death if not treated promptly.

In regions where drug-resistant malaria is prevalent, healthcare providers must carefully monitor patients for treatment failure and adjust the treatment regimen accordingly. For example, in Southeast Asia, multidrug-resistant strains of *P. falciparum* have emerged, necessitating the use of alternative therapies or higher doses of existing drugs.

Public Health Education and Promotion

Public health education is essential for controlling the spread of malaria and ensuring that individuals in endemic areas are aware of the available prevention and treatment options. Education campaigns should focus on encouraging the use of ITNs, promoting the importance of early diagnosis and treatment, and raising awareness about the dangers of self-medication with substandard or counterfeit antimalarial drugs.

In addition to promoting preventive measures, public health education should emphasize the importance of completing the full course of antimalarial treatment. Incomplete or improper treatment can lead to drug resistance, making it more difficult to control malaria in the future. For instance, patients should be informed about the risks of stopping treatment once they start feeling better and the importance of following the prescribed treatment regimen.

10.4.1 Importance of a Balanced Diet

A balanced diet is fundamental to maintaining overall health and well-being, providing the body with the essential nutrients required for its proper functioning. It includes a variety of foods in the right proportions from all food groups, ensuring that the body receives the necessary vitamins, minerals, proteins, carbohydrates, fats, and fiber. A well-balanced diet not only supports physical health but also plays a critical role in mental and emotional well being.

Nutritional Requirements

The human body requires a broad range of nutrients to function optimally. Each nutrient plays a specific role in maintaining health, and deficiencies or excesses can lead to various health problems. For instance:

- **Carbohydrates** are the body's primary source of energy. Complex carbohydrates, such as those found in whole grains, vegetables, and legumes, provide sustained energy and are rich in fiber, which aids in digestion and helps maintain a healthy weight.
- **Proteins** are essential for the growth, repair, and maintenance of body tissues. They are also crucial for the production of enzymes, hormones,

and other vital molecules. A diet rich in high-quality proteins, such as lean meats, fish, eggs, dairy products, legumes, and nuts, ensures that the body can repair itself and maintain muscle mass.

- **Fats** are necessary for the absorption of fat-soluble vitamins (A, D, E, and K) and for providing a concentrated source of energy. Healthy fats, such as those found in olive oil, avocados, nuts, and fatty fish, contribute to heart health and brain function. However, it is important to limit the intake of saturated and trans fats, which are associated with an increased risk of cardiovascular disease.
- **Vitamins and minerals** play a variety of roles in the body, from supporting immune function to aiding in the production of energy and maintaining bone health. For example, calcium and vitamin D are essential for strong bones, while vitamin C supports the immune system and aids in the absorption of iron.
- **Fiber** is crucial for digestive health, helping to prevent constipation and reduce the risk of colon cancer. It also plays a role in controlling blood sugar levels and lowering cholesterol.

Health Benefits of a Balanced Diet

A balanced diet is associated with numerous health benefits, including the prevention of chronic diseases such as heart disease, diabetes, and cancer. For example, a diet rich in fruits, vegetables, whole grains, and lean proteins has been shown to lower blood pressure, reduce cholesterol levels, and decrease the risk of cardiovascular disease. Similarly, consuming a diet high in fiber and low in refined sugars helps regulate blood glucose levels, reducing the risk of type 2 diabetes.

In addition to preventing chronic diseases, a balanced diet supports overall energy levels and mental health. Proper nutrition is linked to improved cognitive function, mood stability, and a reduced risk of mental health disorders such as depression and anxiety. For instance, omega-3 fatty acids, found in fatty fish like salmon and mackerel, are known to support brain health and have been associated with a lower risk of depression.

Preventing Deficiency Disorders

A balanced diet is essential for preventing deficiency disorders, which occur when the body does not get enough of a specific nutrient. Common deficiency disorders include:

- **Iron deficiency anemia**: This condition results from inadequate iron intake and is characterized by fatigue, weakness, and pale skin. It is particularly common among women of childbearing age, pregnant women, and young children. Including iron-rich foods such as red meat, poultry, fish, lentils, and fortified cereals in the diet can help prevent this condition.
- **Vitamin D deficiency**: This deficiency can lead to rickets in children and osteomalacia or osteoporosis in adults, conditions that cause weakened bones and increased risk of fractures. Vitamin D can be obtained from sunlight exposure, fortified foods, and foods such as fatty fish and egg yolks.
- **Vitamin A deficiency**: This condition can lead to night blindness and an increased risk of infections. It is particularly prevalent in developing countries where access to vitamin A-rich foods, such as carrots, sweet potatoes, and leafy green vegetables, may be limited.
- **Iodine deficiency**: Iodine is essential for thyroid function, and its deficiency can lead to goiter and other thyroid-related disorders. Consuming iodized salt and foods like dairy products, fish, and eggs can help prevent iodine deficiency.

Public health initiatives aimed at promoting a balanced diet often focus on increasing awareness of the importance of diverse food intake and the role of specific nutrients in preventing deficiency disorders. For example, educational campaigns may encourage the consumption of a variety of fruits and vegetables, the use of iodized salt, and the fortification of foods with essential vitamins and minerals.

10.4.2 Treatment and Prevention of Deficiency Disorders

Deficiency disorders arise when the body lacks essential nutrients required for its optimal functioning. These deficiencies can lead to a range of health problems, affecting everything from energy levels and immune function to bone health and cognitive abilities. The treatment and prevention of deficiency disorders are crucial components of public health strategies, particularly in regions where malnutrition is prevalent. Addressing these issues involves not only dietary changes but also supplementation, fortification, and public health education.

Common Deficiency Disorders and Their Treatment

Several common deficiency disorders are of particular concern globally, each requiring specific approaches to treatment:

- **Iron Deficiency Anemia**: This is one of the most widespread nutritional deficiencies, particularly affecting women and children. Iron deficiency anemia is characterized by fatigue, weakness, and pallor due to the body's inability to produce enough healthy red blood cells. Treatment typically involves iron supplementation in the form of ferrous sulfate tablets or liquid, along with dietary changes to include more iron-rich foods such as red meat, poultry, fish, lentils, and fortified cereals. In some cases, vitamin C supplements are recommended to enhance iron absorption.
- **Vitamin D Deficiency**: Vitamin D is crucial for calcium absorption and bone health. Deficiency can lead to rickets in children and osteomalacia or osteoporosis in adults, resulting in weak bones and an increased risk of fractures. Treatment usually involves vitamin D supplements, particularly in regions with limited sunlight exposure, where individuals are at higher risk. Additionally, increasing the intake of vitamin D-rich foods, such as fatty fish, fortified dairy products, and egg yolks, is recommended. For those with severe deficiency, high-dose vitamin D therapy under medical supervision may be necessary.
- **Vitamin A Deficiency**: Vitamin A is essential for vision, immune function, and cell growth. Deficiency can cause night blindness and increase susceptibility to infections. In severe cases, it can lead to xerophthalmia, a condition that can result in blindness. Treatment involves high-dose vitamin A supplements, especially in areas where deficiency is common. Preventive measures include promoting the consumption of vitamin A-rich foods like carrots, sweet potatoes, and dark leafy greens, and the fortification of staple foods with vitamin A.
- **Iodine Deficiency**: Iodine is necessary for thyroid hormone production, which regulates metabolism and is critical for brain development in infants and children. Iodine deficiency can lead to goiter, hypothyroidism, and cognitive impairments. Treatment includes iodine supplementation, often in the form of iodized salt, which is a widely used public health intervention. In areas where iodine deficiency is endemic, efforts to ensure universal access to iodized salt are crucial. Additionally, public health campaigns may promote the consumption of iodine-rich foods such as dairy products, seafood, and eggs.

Prevention Strategies for Deficiency Disorders

Preventing deficiency disorders requires a multifaceted approach that combines dietary improvements, supplementation, food fortification, and education.

- **Dietary Improvements**: Encouraging the consumption of a varied and balanced diet is fundamental to preventing nutrient deficiencies. Public health initiatives often focus on promoting the intake of diverse food groups, including fruits, vegetables, whole grains, proteins, and dairy. For example, educational programs might teach communities about the importance of including sources of iron, calcium, and vitamins in their daily meals to prevent deficiencies.
- **Supplementation Programs**: In regions where specific deficiencies are prevalent, targeted supplementation programs are essential. For example, iron and folic acid supplements are often provided to pregnant women to prevent anemia, while vitamin D supplements may be recommended for individuals at risk of deficiency due to limited sun exposure. These programs are particularly important in vulnerable populations, such as children, pregnant women, and the elderly.
- **Food Fortification**: Fortification of staple foods with essential nutrients is an effective public health strategy to combat widespread deficiencies. For instance, fortifying wheat flour with iron and folic acid, or adding vitamin A to cooking oil and sugar, has proven successful in reducing deficiency rates in many countries. Fortification ensures that even populations with limited access to a variety of foods receive essential nutrients through their regular diet.
- **Public Health Education**: Educating the public about the importance of a balanced diet and the risks of nutrient deficiencies is crucial for prevention. Health promotion campaigns can raise awareness about the symptoms of common deficiencies and encourage individuals to seek early treatment. For example, campaigns might focus on educating parents about the signs of iron deficiency anemia in children or the importance of vitamin D for bone health. Additionally, teaching communities how to prepare and store foods to preserve their nutritional value can help prevent deficiencies.

Monitoring and Evaluation

Effective prevention and treatment of deficiency disorders also require ongoing monitoring and evaluation. Healthcare providers should regularly screen at-risk populations for signs of nutrient deficiencies and track the effectiveness of interventions such as supplementation and fortification programs. For example, blood tests to measure hemoglobin levels can help identify iron deficiency anemia early, allowing for timely treatment. Similarly, monitoring the prevalence of goiter in school-aged children can indicate the effectiveness of iodine supplementation efforts.

10.5.1 Methods of Family Planning

Family planning is a critical aspect of public health that enables individuals and couples to determine the number and spacing of their children, thereby contributing to the health and well-being of families and communities. The methods of family planning available today are diverse, catering to different needs, preferences, and health conditions. These methods can be broadly categorized into natural methods, barrier methods, hormonal methods, intrauterine devices (IUDs), sterilization, and emergency contraception. Each method has its advantages, disadvantages, and suitability depending on the individual's or couple's circumstances.

Natural Methods

Natural methods of family planning involve understanding and tracking the body's natural fertility signals to avoid or achieve pregnancy. These methods do not involve the use of drugs or devices, making them free of side effects and cost-effective. However, they require careful monitoring and a high level of commitment.

- **Fertility Awareness-Based Methods (FABMs)**: FABMs involve tracking the menstrual cycle and identifying the fertile window when pregnancy is most likely to occur. Techniques include monitoring basal body temperature, cervical mucus, and calendar calculations. For example, the symptothermal method combines these indicators to predict ovulation. FABMs can be effective when used correctly, but they require thorough education and consistency.
- **Withdrawal (Coitus Interruptus)**: This method involves withdrawing the penis from the vagina before ejaculation to prevent sperm from entering the uterus. While it is simple and does not require any tools or medications, it is less reliable due to the risk of pre-ejaculate fluid containing sperm and the potential for timing errors.

Barrier Methods

Barrier methods prevent sperm from reaching the egg, thereby preventing fertilization. These methods are generally easy to use and have few side effects.

- **Condoms**: Condoms are one of the most widely used barrier methods. They come in male and female versions, with male condoms being worn over the penis and female condoms inserted into the vagina. Condoms also provide protection against sexually transmitted infections (STIs), making them a dual-purpose method. For example, latex male condoms are highly effective when used correctly, with a typical use failure rate of about 13%.
- **Diaphragms and Cervical Caps**: These are dome-shaped devices inserted into the vagina to cover the cervix, blocking sperm from entering the uterus. They are often used with spermicides to increase effectiveness. However, they require correct insertion and removal, and their effectiveness depends on consistent and proper use.
- **Spermicides**: Spermicides are chemicals that immobilize or kill sperm. They are available in various forms, such as gels, creams, foams, and suppositories. While they can be used alone, spermicides are more effective when used in combination with other barrier methods, like condoms or diaphragms.

Hormonal Methods

Hormonal methods of family planning work by altering a woman's hormonal balance to prevent ovulation, thicken cervical mucus, or thin the lining of the uterus to prevent pregnancy. These methods are highly effective when used correctly but require adherence to the prescribed schedule.

- **Oral Contraceptives (The Pill)**: Oral contraceptives contain synthetic hormones, either a combination of estrogen and progestin or progestin alone. The combination pill prevents ovulation, while the progestin-only pill primarily thickens cervical mucus and thins the uterine lining. For example, the typical use failure rate for combination pills is about 7%, largely due to missed doses.
- **Injectable Contraceptives**: Injectable contraceptives, such as Depo-Provera, are administered every three months and provide long-lasting pregnancy prevention by releasing progestin into the bloodstream. They are highly effective with a typical use failure rate of about 4%.

- **Implants**: Contraceptive implants are small, flexible rods inserted under the skin of the upper arm, releasing progestin to prevent pregnancy for up to three years. For instance, the contraceptive implant Nexplanon is over 99% effective, with fewer than 1 in 100 women getting pregnant each year.
- **Patches and Vaginal Rings**: The contraceptive patch is worn on the skin and releases hormones similar to those in the pill, while the vaginal ring is inserted into the vagina and releases hormones over a three-week period. Both methods require regular replacement to maintain effectiveness.

Intrauterine Devices (IUDs)

IUDs are small, T-shaped devices inserted into the uterus by a healthcare provider. They are long-acting, reversible contraceptives that can prevent pregnancy for several years.

- **Copper IUDs**: Copper IUDs, such as Paragard, release copper ions, which are toxic to sperm, thereby preventing fertilization. They can be effective for up to 10 years and are a hormone-free option. The failure rate is less than 1%.
- **Hormonal IUDs**: Hormonal IUDs, such as Mirena and Kyleena, release progestin to thicken cervical mucus and thin the uterine lining, preventing pregnancy for 3 to 5 years. These IUDs also reduce menstrual bleeding and cramps, providing additional benefits for some women.

Sterilization

Sterilization is a permanent method of family planning for individuals or couples who do not wish to have more children. It involves surgical procedures to block or seal the fallopian tubes in women or the vas deferens in men, preventing the sperm and egg from meeting.

- **Tubal Ligation**: Tubal ligation, commonly known as "getting your tubes tied," is a surgical procedure in which the fallopian tubes are cut, tied, or sealed to prevent eggs from reaching the uterus. It is highly effective, with a failure rate of less than 1%, but it is generally considered irreversible.
- **Vasectomy**: A vasectomy is a surgical procedure for men that involves cutting or sealing the vas deferens to prevent sperm from entering the

semen. It is also highly effective and is less invasive than tubal ligation. Vasectomies are considered permanent, though reversals are sometimes possible but not guaranteed.

Emergency Contraception

Emergency contraception is used to prevent pregnancy after unprotected sex or contraceptive failure. It is not intended for regular use but as a backup method.

- **Emergency Contraceptive Pills (ECPs)**: ECPs, often referred to as the "morning-after pill," contain higher doses of hormones found in regular birth control pills. They are most effective when taken within 72 hours of unprotected sex. For example, the levonorgestrel pill (Plan B) reduces the risk of pregnancy by 89% when taken within the recommended time frame.
- **Copper IUD**: The copper IUD can also be used as emergency contraception if inserted within five days of unprotected sex. It is more than 99% effective and provides ongoing contraception for up to 10 years.

10.5.2 Role of Pharmacist in Family Planning

Pharmacists play a vital role in family planning by providing accessible, accurate, and confidential information and services to individuals and couples seeking to manage their reproductive health. As healthcare professionals who are often the first point of contact for many people, pharmacists are uniquely positioned to offer counseling on various family planning methods, guide appropriate contraceptive choices, and ensure the safe and effective use of these methods. Their involvement is crucial in both urban and rural settings, where access to healthcare may vary, making their contributions indispensable to public health.

Counseling and Education

One of the primary roles of pharmacists in family planning is to provide counseling and education. Pharmacists are responsible for informing individuals and couples about the different contraceptive options available, including their benefits, risks, and correct usage. This education is tailored to the individual's needs, taking into account factors such as age, health status, sexual activity, and future reproductive plans.

For instance, a pharmacist might counsel a young woman on the use of oral contraceptives, explaining how to take the pills correctly, what to do if a dose is missed, and potential side effects. The pharmacist might also discuss the importance of using condoms to protect against sexually transmitted infections (STIs) alongside oral contraceptives, which do not offer such protection. In addition, pharmacists can provide information about emergency contraception for situations where primary contraception may have failed.

Accessibility and Distribution of Contraceptives

Pharmacists significantly contribute to making contraceptives more accessible, especially in areas where other healthcare services may be limited. In many countries, pharmacies are authorized to dispense a range of contraceptive products, including condoms, oral contraceptives, injectables, and emergency contraception, often without the need for a doctor's prescription. This accessibility helps reduce barriers to obtaining contraception, particularly for those who may feel uncomfortable discussing their reproductive health with a physician or who live in areas with limited healthcare facilities.

For example, a woman seeking emergency contraception after unprotected intercourse can quickly obtain it from a pharmacist, who can also provide guidance on its use and discuss future contraceptive options to prevent similar situations. This ease of access is crucial in preventing unintended pregnancies and allowing individuals to take control of their reproductive health.

Monitoring and Follow-Up

Pharmacists also play a role in monitoring and follow-up to ensure that individuals are using their chosen contraceptive methods effectively and safely. This includes addressing any side effects, answering questions, and ensuring that the individual understands how to use the method correctly. For instance, a pharmacist might follow up with a patient who has started using a hormonal contraceptive to check for any adverse effects, such as nausea or headaches, and provide solutions or refer the patient to a physician if necessary.

Moreover, pharmacists can help ensure continuity of care by reminding patients when it is time to renew their prescriptions or receive their next dose of a contraceptive method, such as an injectable. This ongoing support helps improve adherence to family planning methods and reduces the risk of contraceptive failure.

Advocacy and Public Health Promotion

Pharmacists also serve as advocates for family planning and reproductive health within their communities. They can participate in public health campaigns aimed at raising awareness about the importance of family planning, the availability of contraceptive options, and the role of contraception in preventing unintended pregnancies and improving maternal and child health.

For example, pharmacists might be involved in organizing community workshops or informational sessions on reproductive health, where they can educate the public about the various methods of contraception and address common misconceptions. These efforts contribute to a more informed community, where individuals feel empowered to make choices about their reproductive health.

Confidentiality and Non-Judgmental Support

An important aspect of the pharmacist's role in family planning is providing confidential and non-judgmental support. Pharmacists must create a safe and respectful environment where individuals feel comfortable seeking advice and services related to family planning. This is particularly important in cultures or communities where discussing sexual and reproductive health is considered taboo or where individuals might face stigma for seeking contraception.

For example, a pharmacist should maintain the confidentiality of a teenage girl seeking birth control, ensuring that her privacy is protected and providing her with the necessary information and support without judgment. This approach encourages more people to seek the services they need, leading to better health outcomes.

Integration with Other Healthcare Services

Pharmacists often work collaboratively with other healthcare providers, such as physicians, nurses, and public health workers, to provide comprehensive family planning services. This integration ensures that patients receive well-rounded care that addresses all aspects of their reproductive health. For instance, a pharmacist might refer a patient to a gynecologist for further evaluation if they experience complications with a contraceptive method, ensuring that the patient receives appropriate care and support.

ELEVEN

Responding to Symptoms of Minor Ailments

11.1.1 Pain Management

Pain is one of the most common symptoms prompting individuals to seek medical advice or over-the-counter (OTC) remedies. It is a complex physiological response to stimuli that can be both acute and chronic, with various underlying causes such as injury, inflammation, or nerve damage. Understanding the pathophysiology of pain and the appropriate drug therapy is crucial for effective management, particularly in the context of minor ailments where patients often rely on OTC medications.

Pathophysiology of Pain

Pain is generally classified into two major categories: nociceptive and neuropathic pain. **Nociceptive pain** is a response to tissue damage or injury, where pain receptors (nociceptors) are activated by stimuli such as mechanical pressure, heat, or chemical irritants. This type of pain is typically acute, localized, and can be further categorized into somatic (originating from skin, muscles, or bones) and visceral (originating from internal organs). For example, a sprained ankle or a headache is usually nociceptive pain.

On the other hand, **neuropathic pain** arises from damage to the nervous system itself, either due to injury, disease, or dysfunction of the nerves. This type of pain is often chronic and can be more challenging to treat. Neuropathic pain may present as burning, tingling, or shooting sensations, as seen in conditions like diabetic neuropathy or post-herpetic neuralgia.

Drug Therapy for Pain Management

The management of pain involves the use of various pharmacological agents, tailored to the type, severity, and underlying cause of the pain. The most commonly used classes of drugs for pain management in minor ailments include nonsteroidal anti-inflammatory drugs (NSAIDs), acetaminophen (paracetamol), and topical analgesics.

- **Nonsteroidal Anti-Inflammatory Drugs (NSAIDs)**: NSAIDs, such as ibuprofen, aspirin, and naproxen, are widely used for managing mild to moderate pain, particularly when inflammation is a contributing factor. These drugs work by inhibiting the enzyme cyclooxygenase (COX), which is involved in the production of prostaglandins—compounds that mediate inflammation and pain. For instance, ibuprofen is commonly recommended for conditions like headaches, menstrual cramps, and musculoskeletal pain due to its anti-inflammatory and analgesic properties. However, NSAIDs can cause gastrointestinal irritation, renal impairment, and an increased risk of cardiovascular events, especially with long-term use.
- **Acetaminophen (Paracetamol)**: Acetaminophen is another popular analgesic used for mild to moderate pain relief, such as in cases of headaches, osteoarthritis, and fever. Unlike NSAIDs, acetaminophen lacks anti-inflammatory properties and primarily acts centrally in the brain to inhibit the synthesis of prostaglandins, which reduces the perception of pain. Acetaminophen is generally well-tolerated and has a favorable safety profile when used within the recommended dosage limits. However, exceeding the maximum daily dose can lead to hepatotoxicity, making it essential for patients to be aware of the risks associated with overdose.
- **Topical Analgesics**: Topical analgesics, such as creams, gels, and patches containing ingredients like menthol, capsaicin, or diclofenac, are used for localized pain relief. These products work by providing direct pain relief to the affected area without the systemic side effects associated with oral medications. For example, capsaicin cream is often used to relieve neuropathic pain by depleting substance P, a neuropeptide involved in transmitting pain signals to the brain. Topical NSAIDs, like diclofenac gel, are also effective for treating joint and muscle pain with a lower risk of gastrointestinal side effects compared to oral NSAIDs.

Combination Therapies

In some cases, a combination of different analgesics may be recommended to enhance pain relief and reduce the risk of side effects. For instance, a combination of acetaminophen and an NSAID may provide better pain control than either drug alone, especially in conditions like tension headaches or dental pain. Additionally, combining an analgesic with an adjunct therapy, such as a muscle relaxant or an anti-anxiety medication, may be beneficial in cases where muscle tension or anxiety contributes to the pain.

Patient Education and Counseling

Pharmacists play a critical role in educating patients about the appropriate use of pain medications, including correct dosing, potential side effects, and the importance of adhering to the recommended treatment regimen. For example, patients should be advised not to exceed the maximum daily dose of acetaminophen (typically 4,000 mg for adults) to avoid liver damage. Similarly, patients using NSAIDs should be informed about the risks of gastrointestinal bleeding and advised to take the medication with food or use a gastroprotective agent, such as a proton pump inhibitor, if they are at high risk.

In addition to pharmacological treatment, pharmacists can provide advice on non-drug approaches to pain management, such as rest, ice or heat application, physical therapy, and stress reduction techniques. For instance, applying an ice pack to an acute injury can help reduce inflammation and pain in the early stages, while heat therapy may be more beneficial for chronic muscle pain.

11.1.2 Gastrointestinal Disturbances

Gastrointestinal (GI) disturbances are common complaints that can range from mild discomfort to more severe symptoms, affecting various parts of the digestive system. These disturbances include conditions such as indigestion (dyspepsia), heartburn (acid reflux), diarrhea, constipation, and bloating. Understanding the pathophysiology of these conditions and the appropriate drug therapy is crucial for effective management, especially in the context of minor ailments that are often self-treated with over-the-counter (OTC) medications.

Pathophysiology of Gastrointestinal Disturbances

The GI tract is a complex system responsible for the digestion and absorption of food, as well as the elimination of waste. Disturbances in this system can arise from various factors, including dietary habits, stress, infections, and underlying medical conditions.

- **Indigestion (Dyspepsia)**: Indigestion is characterized by a feeling of discomfort or pain in the upper abdomen, often accompanied by bloating, nausea, and belching. It can result from overeating, eating too quickly, or consuming fatty or spicy foods. In some cases, dyspepsia may be associated with gastroesophageal reflux disease (GERD), peptic ulcers, or Helicobacter pylori infection.
- **Heartburn (Acid Reflux)**: Heartburn occurs when stomach acid flows back into the esophagus, causing a burning sensation in the chest. This reflux of acid can be triggered by certain foods, such as citrus fruits, chocolate, caffeine, and alcohol, as well as by lying down shortly after eating. Chronic acid reflux can lead to GERD, a more severe condition requiring medical attention.
- **Diarrhea**: Diarrhea is characterized by frequent, loose, or watery stools. It can be caused by infections (bacterial, viral, or parasitic), food intolerances, medications, or chronic conditions such as irritable bowel syndrome (IBS). Diarrhea can lead to dehydration, electrolyte imbalances, and, in severe cases, malnutrition.
- **Constipation**: Constipation is the infrequent or difficult passage of stools, often accompanied by abdominal discomfort. It can result from a diet low in fiber, inadequate fluid intake, lack of physical activity, or certain medications (e.g., opioids, antacids containing aluminum). Chronic constipation may also be a symptom of underlying conditions such as IBS or hypothyroidism.
- **Bloating**: Bloating is the sensation of fullness or swelling in the abdomen, often caused by the accumulation of gas or fluid in the GI tract. It can result from overeating, swallowing air, consuming gas-producing foods (e.g., beans, broccoli, carbonated beverages), or disorders like IBS.

Drug Therapy for Gastrointestinal Disturbances

The management of GI disturbances often involves the use of OTC medications tailored to the specific symptoms and underlying causes. These medications include antacids, proton pump inhibitors (PPIs), H2 receptor antagonists, antidiarrheals, laxatives, and antiflatulents.

- **Antacids**: Antacids are commonly used to neutralize stomach acid and provide quick relief from heartburn and indigestion. They contain compounds such as magnesium hydroxide, aluminum hydroxide, calcium carbonate, or sodium bicarbonate. For example, calcium carbonate (found in products like Tums) provides rapid relief by neutralizing acid in the stomach. However, long-term use of antacids can lead to side effects such as constipation (with aluminum-based antacids) or diarrhea (with magnesium-based antacids).

- **Proton Pump Inhibitors (PPIs) and H2 Receptor Antagonists**: PPIs, such as omeprazole and esomeprazole, are more potent acid suppressors used to treat frequent heartburn and GERD by inhibiting the proton pumps in the stomach lining that produce acid. H2 receptor antagonists, like ranitidine and famotidine, reduce acid production by blocking histamine receptors on stomach cells. These medications are effective for longer-term management of acid-related conditions but should be used with caution due to potential risks, such as nutrient malabsorption and increased susceptibility to infections with prolonged use.
- **Antidiarrheals**: Medications such as loperamide (Imodium) slow intestinal motility, allowing more water to be absorbed from the stool and reducing the frequency of bowel movements. Antidiarrheals are useful in managing acute diarrhea, especially when caused by non-infectious factors like IBS. However, they should be avoided in cases of infectious diarrhea, as they can prolong the presence of pathogens in the gut.
- **Laxatives**: Laxatives are used to relieve constipation and are available in several forms, including bulk-forming agents (e.g., psyllium), stool softeners (e.g., docusate sodium), osmotic laxatives (e.g., polyethylene glycol), and stimulant laxatives (e.g., bisacodyl). Bulk-forming agents work by absorbing water and increasing stool bulk, while osmotic laxatives draw water into the bowel to soften stools. Stimulant laxatives, which stimulate bowel contractions, should be used with caution to avoid dependency.
- **Antiflatulents**: Simethicone is a commonly used antiflatulent that helps reduce gas in the digestive tract by breaking up gas bubbles, making them easier to pass. It is often used to relieve bloating and discomfort associated with gas and can be found in products like Gas-X.

Patient Education and Counseling

Effective management of GI disturbances involves not only the appropriate use of medications but also lifestyle and dietary modifications.

Pharmacists play a crucial role in educating patients about these changes, which can help prevent the recurrence of symptoms.

For example, patients with frequent heartburn should be advised to avoid trigger foods, eat smaller meals, avoid lying down after eating, and maintain a healthy weight. Those prone to constipation may benefit from increasing their intake of dietary fiber, drinking plenty of fluids, and engaging in regular physical activity.

Pharmacists should also counsel patients on the proper use of OTC medications, including the importance of not exceeding the recommended doses and understanding the potential side effects. For instance, patients using PPIs or H2 receptor antagonists for extended periods should be aware of the risks associated with long-term use and be encouraged to consult a healthcare provider if symptoms persist.

11.1.3 Pyrexia

Pyrexia, commonly known as fever, is a temporary elevation in body temperature often associated with an underlying infection, inflammation, or other medical conditions. Fever is a common symptom in various minor ailments, ranging from viral infections like the common cold to bacterial infections and inflammatory disorders. While fever is a natural defense mechanism of the body, aimed at fighting off infections, it can also cause discomfort and require management, especially when it is high or prolonged.

Pathophysiology of Pyrexia

Fever occurs when the body's thermoregulatory set-point in the hypothalamus is reset to a higher level due to the presence of pyrogens—substances that induce fever. Pyrogens can be exogenous, such as bacteria, viruses, and toxins, or endogenous, such as cytokines released by the body in response to infection or inflammation.

When pyrogens are detected, the hypothalamus increases the set-point temperature, triggering mechanisms that raise body temperature. These mechanisms include shivering to generate heat, vasoconstriction to reduce heat loss through the skin, and behavioral changes like seeking warmth. As the body temperature rises to the new set-point, the person may feel cold and experience chills until the desired temperature is reached. Once the fever subsides, the set-point returns to normal, and the body begins to cool down, often resulting in sweating.

Fever is generally classified based on its severity:

- **Low-grade fever**: 37.2°C to 38°C (99°F to 100.4°F)
- **Moderate fever**: 38.1°C to 39.4°C (100.5°F to 103°F)
- **High fever**: 39.5°C to 41°C (103.1°F to 105.8°F)
- **Hyperpyrexia**: Above 41°C (105.8°F), which is a medical emergency and requires immediate intervention.

Drug Therapy for Pyrexia

The management of fever typically involves the use of antipyretic medications, which help lower body temperature and relieve discomfort. The most commonly used antipyretics are acetaminophen (paracetamol) and nonsteroidal anti-inflammatory drugs (NSAIDs) such as ibuprofen.

- **Acetaminophen (Paracetamol)**: Acetaminophen is one of the most widely used antipyretics due to its effectiveness and relatively low risk of side effects when used at the recommended doses. It works by inhibiting the production of prostaglandins in the brain, which are involved in the fever response. Acetaminophen is often the first-line treatment for fever in both adults and children, as it is gentle on the stomach and does not cause gastrointestinal irritation. The typical dose for adults is 500 to 1000 mg every 4 to 6 hours, with a maximum daily dose of 4,000 mg. However, it is important to avoid overdose, as excessive intake can lead to severe liver damage.
- **Ibuprofen**: Ibuprofen is another effective antipyretic that also provides anti-inflammatory and analgesic benefits. It works by inhibiting the cyclooxygenase (COX) enzymes, which are involved in the production of prostaglandins. Ibuprofen is particularly useful when fever is accompanied by inflammation or pain, such as in cases of viral infections, muscle aches, or headaches. The typical dose for adults is 200 to 400 mg every 4 to 6 hours, with a maximum daily dose of 1,200 mg for over-the-counter use. While ibuprofen is effective, it should be used with caution in individuals with gastrointestinal issues, kidney problems, or those at risk of cardiovascular events.
- **Aspirin**: Aspirin is an older antipyretic and anti-inflammatory agent that is still used in some cases, particularly for its cardiovascular benefits. However, it is generally not recommended for fever management in children and adolescents due to the risk of Reye's syndrome, a rare but serious condition that causes swelling in the liver and brain.

Non-Pharmacological Management

In addition to drug therapy, non-pharmacological measures can help manage fever and provide comfort. These measures include:

- **Hydration**: Fever increases the body's fluid loss through sweating, so it is important to stay well-hydrated. Drinking plenty of fluids such as water, oral rehydration solutions, or clear broths can help prevent dehydration.
- **Rest**: Resting allows the body to conserve energy and focus on fighting the underlying infection or inflammation that is causing the fever.
- **Cool Compresses**: Applying a cool, damp cloth to the forehead, wrists, or the back of the neck can help reduce body temperature and provide relief from the discomfort associated with fever.
- **Light Clothing**: Wearing light and loose-fitting clothing and using light bedding can help the body dissipate heat more effectively.

Patient Education and Counseling

Pharmacists play a critical role in educating patients and caregivers about the appropriate use of antipyretics and the management of fever. It is important to counsel patients on the correct dosing, frequency, and potential side effects of antipyretic medications. For example, parents should be advised to use the correct dosing device (e.g., a dosing syringe) when administering acetaminophen or ibuprofen to children, as incorrect dosing can lead to under-treatment or overdose.

Patients should also be informed about when to seek medical attention for fever. For instance, medical evaluation is recommended if a fever persists for more than three days, is very high (above 39.4°C or 103°F), or is accompanied by other concerning symptoms such as severe headache, rash, stiff neck, shortness of breath, or confusion.

11.1.4 Ophthalmic Symptoms

Ophthalmic symptoms, including red eyes, itching, tearing, dryness, and blurred vision, are common minor ailments that can significantly affect an individual's quality of life. These symptoms can result from a variety of causes, ranging from environmental irritants and allergies to infections and eye strain. Understanding the pathophysiology behind these symptoms and the appropriate drug therapy is essential for effective management, particularly when patients seek over-the-counter (OTC) remedies.

Pathophysiology of Ophthalmic Symptoms

The eye is a delicate organ with several components, including the cornea, conjunctiva, sclera, and tear film, each playing a crucial role in maintaining ocular health and vision. Ophthalmic symptoms often arise when these structures are irritated, inflamed, or infected.

- **Red Eye (Conjunctival Hyperemia)**: Redness of the eye occurs when the blood vessels in the conjunctiva become dilated, often due to irritation, infection, or inflammation. Common causes include conjunctivitis (pink eye), which can be viral, bacterial, or allergic in nature. Environmental factors like smoke, dust, and prolonged exposure to screens can also cause red eyes.
- **Itching and Tearing**: Itching is a common symptom of allergic conjunctivitis, where the eyes react to allergens such as pollen, pet dander, or dust mites. Tearing, or excessive lacrimation, can accompany itching and may be exacerbated by exposure to irritants, dry eye syndrome, or infections.
- **Dry Eye Syndrome**: Dry eye occurs when the eyes do not produce enough tears or when the tear film is of poor quality, leading to discomfort, irritation, and sometimes blurred vision. This condition can be caused by environmental factors (e.g., dry air, wind), prolonged screen use, aging, certain medications (e.g., antihistamines, antidepressants), and systemic conditions like Sjogren's syndrome.
- **Blurred Vision**: Blurred vision can result from various factors, including refractive errors (e.g., myopia, hyperopia), cataracts, corneal abrasions, or infections like keratitis. In minor ailments, blurred vision is often temporary and may be associated with dry eyes or eye strain.

Drug Therapy for Ophthalmic Symptoms

The treatment of ophthalmic symptoms often involves the use of topical eye drops and ointments, which provide relief by addressing the underlying cause of the symptoms. Commonly used drug therapies include artificial tears, antihistamine eye drops, decongestants, and antibiotic or antiviral eye drops.

- **Artificial Tears**: Artificial tears are a cornerstone of treatment for dry eye syndrome. These eye drops lubricate the eyes, mimicking natural tears and providing relief from dryness, irritation, and discomfort. They are available in various formulations, including preservative-free options for individuals with sensitive eyes. For example, artificial tears containing carboxymethylcellulose or hyaluronic acid can help maintain moisture on the eye's surface, improving comfort and reducing the risk of further irritation.

- **Antihistamine Eye Drops**: Antihistamine eye drops are commonly used to treat allergic conjunctivitis, relieving symptoms such as itching, redness, and tearing. These drops work by blocking histamine receptors in the eye, reducing the allergic response. For instance, ketotifen and olopatadine are popular antihistamine eye drops that provide quick relief from allergic symptoms. Some antihistamine drops also contain mast cell stabilizers, which help prevent the release of histamine and other inflammatory mediators.
- **Decongestant Eye Drops**: Decongestant eye drops, such as those containing naphazoline or tetrahydrozoline, constrict the blood vessels in the conjunctiva, reducing redness and swelling. However, these drops should be used with caution, as prolonged use can lead to rebound redness, where symptoms worsen once the drops are discontinued. Decongestant eye drops are typically recommended for short-term use to relieve redness due to minor irritants.
- **Antibiotic and Antiviral Eye Drops**: In cases of bacterial conjunctivitis or keratitis, antibiotic eye drops are necessary to eliminate the infection and prevent complications. Common antibiotics used include erythromycin, tobramycin, and moxifloxacin. Viral infections, such as those caused by the herpes simplex virus, may require antiviral eye drops like ganciclovir. It is important to note that antibiotic and antiviral treatments should be used under the guidance of a healthcare provider, as incorrect use can lead to resistance or worsening of symptoms.

Non-Pharmacological Management

In addition to drug therapy, non-pharmacological measures can help manage ophthalmic symptoms and prevent recurrence. These measures include:

- **Environmental Modifications**: Reducing exposure to irritants and allergens can help alleviate symptoms. For example, using air purifiers, avoiding smoke, and minimizing time spent in windy or dusty environments can reduce irritation and redness.

- **Proper Eye Hygiene**: Practicing good eye hygiene, such as regular hand washing and avoiding touching the eyes, can prevent the spread of infections. For contact lens wearers, proper lens care and hygiene are essential to prevent complications like infections and corneal ulcers.
- **Cold Compresses**: Applying a cold compress to the eyes can help reduce inflammation and soothe itching or redness, particularly in cases of allergic conjunctivitis or irritation from environmental factors.
- **Frequent Breaks from Screen Time**: For individuals experiencing eye strain or dry eyes due to prolonged screen use, taking regular breaks (e.g., following the 20-20-20 rule: every 20 minutes, look at something 20 feet away for 20 seconds) can help reduce symptoms and prevent further discomfort.

Patient Education and Counseling

Pharmacists play a key role in educating patients about the appropriate use of eye drops and other treatments for ophthalmic symptoms. This includes instructing patients on how to properly administer eye drops, the importance of not sharing eye medications, and when to seek medical attention for more serious or persistent symptoms.

For example, patients should be advised to wash their hands before using eye drops, avoid touching the dropper tip to any surface (including the eye), and follow the prescribed dosing schedule. If symptoms persist or worsen, or if there is severe pain, vision loss, or discharge from the eye, patients should be referred to an eye care professional for further evaluation.

11.1.5 Worm Infestations

Worm infestations, also known as helminthic infections, are a common health concern, particularly in regions with poor sanitation and hygiene practices. These infestations can affect individuals of all ages but are especially prevalent among children. The most common types of worm infestations include roundworms (Ascaris lumbricoides), pinworms (Enterobius vermicularis), hookworms (Ancylostoma duodenale and Necator americanus), and tapeworms (Taenia species). Understanding the pathophysiology of these infestations and the appropriate drug therapy is essential for effective management and prevention.

Pathophysiology of Worm Infestations

Worm infestations typically occur when individuals ingest worm eggs or larvae through contaminated food, water, soil, or by direct contact with infected surfaces. Once inside the body, these parasites can live and reproduce in various parts of the gastrointestinal tract, leading to a range of symptoms depending on the type of worm involved.

- **Roundworms (Ascaris lumbricoides)**: Roundworm infections are transmitted through the ingestion of eggs found in contaminated food or water. The eggs hatch in the intestines, and the larvae migrate through the bloodstream to the lungs, where they mature before returning to the intestines to develop into adult worms. Symptoms of roundworm infection may include abdominal pain, diarrhea, nausea, and, in severe cases, intestinal blockage.
- **Pinworms (Enterobius vermicularis)**: Pinworm infections are highly contagious and commonly spread through direct contact with contaminated surfaces or ingestion of pinworm eggs. The female pinworms migrate to the anal area at night to lay eggs, causing intense itching and discomfort. This leads to scratching, which can spread the eggs to other surfaces and individuals. Pinworm infections are often asymptomatic, but the hallmark symptom is perianal itching, particularly at night.
- **Hookworms (Ancylostoma duodenale and Necator americanus)**: Hookworm larvae penetrate the skin, usually through the feet, when individuals walk barefoot on contaminated soil. The larvae then travel through the bloodstream to the lungs and eventually reach the intestines, where they attach to the intestinal wall and feed on blood. Hookworm infections can cause anemia, fatigue, abdominal pain, and malnutrition, particularly in children.
- **Tapeworms (Taenia species)**: Tapeworm infections are typically acquired through the ingestion of undercooked or contaminated meat containing tapeworm larvae. Once ingested, the larvae develop into adult tapeworms in the intestines, where they can grow to several meters in length. Tapeworm infections may be asymptomatic or cause symptoms such as abdominal discomfort, nausea, and weight loss. In some cases, tapeworm segments may be visible in the stool.

Drug Therapy for Worm Infestations

The treatment of worm infestations involves the use of anthelmintic medications, which are designed to kill or expel the worms from the body. The choice of medication depends on the type of worm involved and the severity of the infestation.

- **Albendazole and Mebendazole**: Albendazole and mebendazole are broad-spectrum anthelmintics commonly used to treat a variety of worm infestations, including roundworms, pinworms, hookworms, and tapeworms. These medications work by inhibiting the worms' ability to absorb glucose, leading to energy depletion and death of the parasite. A single dose of albendazole or mebendazole is often sufficient to treat most worm infections, although a second dose may be needed after two weeks to eliminate any remaining eggs or larvae.
- **Pyrantel Pamoate**: Pyrantel pamoate is another anthelmintic commonly used to treat pinworm, roundworm, and hookworm infections. It works by paralyzing the worms, allowing them to be expelled from the body through the stool. Pyrantel pamoate is available as an over-the-counter medication and is often used in single-dose treatments.
- **Praziquantel**: Praziquantel is the drug of choice for treating tapeworm infections and other trematode infestations. It works by increasing the permeability of the worm's cell membranes to calcium, leading to paralysis and death of the parasite. A single dose of praziquantel is usually effective in treating tapeworm infections, but dosage may vary depending on the specific type of tapeworm.
- **Ivermectin**: Ivermectin is an anthelmintic commonly used to treat strongyloidiasis and other parasitic infections, but it is also effective against some types of roundworms. It works by binding to specific channels in the nerve and muscle cells of the worms, causing paralysis and death. Ivermectin is often used in combination with other anthelmintics for more severe or resistant infections.

Prevention and Patient Education

Preventing worm infestations requires a combination of good hygiene practices, proper sanitation, and education. Pharmacists play a crucial role in educating patients and communities about the importance of these preventive measures.

- **Handwashing**: Regular handwashing with soap and water, particularly before eating and after using the toilet, is essential in preventing the spread of worm infections. Pharmacists should educate patients on the importance of hand hygiene, especially in households with young children.

- **Food Safety**: Ensuring that food, particularly meat and vegetables, is thoroughly cooked and properly handled can prevent the ingestion of worm eggs or larvae. Pharmacists can provide guidance on safe food preparation practices to reduce the risk of infection.
- **Sanitation**: Proper sanitation, including the use of clean toilets and the disposal of human waste in sanitary conditions, is critical in preventing soil contamination with worm eggs or larvae. In areas where hookworm infections are prevalent, encouraging individuals to wear shoes when walking on soil can reduce the risk of skin penetration by hookworm larvae.
- **Regular Deworming**: In regions where worm infestations are common, regular deworming programs, particularly for children, can help reduce the prevalence of these infections. Pharmacists can play a role in promoting and administering these deworming treatments.

Patient Counseling

Pharmacists should counsel patients on the correct use of anthelmintic medications, including the importance of taking the full course of treatment even if symptoms improve. Patients should also be advised to maintain good hygiene practices to prevent reinfection and to seek medical attention if symptoms persist or worsen after treatment.

TWELVE

ESSENTIAL DRUGS CONCEPT AND RATIONAL DRUG THERAPY

12.1 Definition and Importance of Essential Drugs

The concept of essential drugs is a cornerstone of public health policy, aiming to ensure that all individuals have access to the most necessary medications for addressing their health needs. Essential drugs are those that satisfy the priority healthcare needs of the population. They are selected based on evidence of their efficacy, safety, and cost-effectiveness, and are intended to be available at all times, in adequate amounts, in appropriate dosage forms, and at affordable prices.

The World Health Organization (WHO) introduced the Essential Medicines List (EML) in 1977, recognizing that the availability of essential drugs is fundamental to achieving universal health coverage and improving public health outcomes. The EML serves as a guideline for countries to develop their own national lists, tailored to their specific health needs and economic conditions. For instance, the Indian government has adopted the National List of Essential Medicines (NLEM), which is regularly updated to reflect the changing health priorities of the nation.

Importance of Essential Drugs

The essential drugs concept is vital for several reasons, all of which contribute to the overall goal of improving public health and ensuring equitable access to healthcare:

1. **Accessibility and Equity**: Essential drugs are selected to address the most prevalent and significant health problems within a community. By focusing on these priority medications, healthcare systems can ensure that even the most disadvantaged populations have access to the necessary treatments. For example, in low- and middle-income countries, the availability of essential drugs for infectious diseases like malaria, tuberculosis, and HIV/AIDS can significantly reduce morbidity and mortality rates.
2. **Cost-Effectiveness**: By concentrating on a limited list of essential drugs, healthcare systems can optimize the use of limited resources. The selection of cost-effective medications ensures that the most health benefits are achieved with the available funding. This approach allows governments and healthcare providers to manage their budgets more efficiently, making it possible to provide essential medicines to a larger portion of the population. For instance, generic versions of essential drugs are often included in the list to reduce costs while maintaining efficacy.
3. **Rational Drug Use**: The essential drugs list promotes rational drug use by guiding healthcare providers in selecting the most appropriate medications for their patients. This reduces the risk of over-prescribing, inappropriate drug use, and the proliferation of counterfeit or substandard medicines. Rational drug use also minimizes the risk of adverse drug reactions and the development of drug resistance, which is particularly important in the treatment of infectious diseases.
4. **Quality Assurance**: Essential drugs are selected based on rigorous evidence of their safety, efficacy, and quality. This ensures that the drugs included in the list meet high standards and are effective in treating the conditions for which they are prescribed. For example, the WHO prequalification program assesses the quality of essential medicines to ensure that they meet international standards before being included in the EML.
5. **Support for Healthcare Infrastructure**: The availability of essential drugs supports the functioning of healthcare systems, particularly in resource-limited settings. By ensuring that these drugs are available at all levels of healthcare, from primary care clinics to tertiary hospitals, healthcare systems can provide comprehensive care to patients. This

also helps in building trust in the healthcare system, as patients are more likely to seek care when they know that effective treatments are available.

6. **Guidance for Policy and Procurement**: The essential drugs list serves as a guideline for national health policies and procurement practices. Governments and healthcare institutions use the list to inform their purchasing decisions, ensuring that resources are allocated to the most critical medications. This also helps in negotiating better prices with pharmaceutical companies, as bulk purchasing of essential drugs can lead to significant cost savings.

12.2.1 Role of Community Pharmacist

Community pharmacists play a crucial role in the implementation of rational drug therapy, ensuring that patients receive medications that are appropriate, effective, safe, and affordable. As accessible healthcare professionals, community pharmacists are often the first point of contact for patients seeking advice on medication use. Their involvement is vital in promoting the principles of rational drug therapy, which aims to optimize the therapeutic outcomes of drug treatment while minimizing the risks of adverse effects and ensuring cost-effectiveness.

Medication Counseling and Patient Education

One of the primary roles of community pharmacists in rational drug therapy is to provide comprehensive medication counseling and patient education. This involves explaining how to use prescribed medications correctly, including the dosage, frequency, and duration of treatment. Pharmacists also educate patients about potential side effects, drug interactions, and the importance of adherence to the prescribed regimen. For example, a pharmacist might counsel a patient on the need to take antibiotics for the full prescribed course, even if symptoms improve, to prevent the development of antibiotic resistance.

Pharmacists also play a key role in helping patients understand the importance of taking medications as directed, particularly for chronic conditions such as hypertension, diabetes, and asthma. By providing clear and accurate information, pharmacists empower patients to take an active role in managing their health, leading to better therapeutic outcomes and a reduced likelihood of medication errors.

Ensuring Appropriate Drug Selection

Community pharmacists are responsible for ensuring that the medications prescribed to patients are appropriate for their condition. This involves reviewing prescriptions to verify that the drug, dosage, and duration of treatment are suitable for the patient's age, weight, and medical history. Pharmacists are trained to detect potential drug interactions, contraindications, and dosing errors, and they can collaborate with prescribing physicians to resolve any issues.

For instance, if a pharmacist notices that a patient has been prescribed a medication that interacts with another drug the patient is already taking, they can contact the prescribing physician to discuss alternative options. This collaborative approach helps prevent adverse drug reactions and ensures that patients receive the most appropriate therapy for their condition.

Promotion of Generic Medications

Another important aspect of the pharmacist's role in rational drug therapy is the promotion of generic medications as cost-effective alternatives to brand-name drugs. Generic medications contain the same active ingredients as their branded counterparts and are equally effective, but they are often available at a lower cost. By recommending generics, pharmacists help reduce the financial burden on patients and healthcare systems while ensuring that patients have access to necessary treatments.

For example, a pharmacist might suggest a generic version of a commonly prescribed medication for hypertension, explaining to the patient that it is just as effective as the brand-name version but more affordable. This not only helps patients manage their health more economically but also contributes to the overall sustainability of the healthcare system.

Adherence Monitoring and Follow-Up

Monitoring patient adherence to prescribed medications is a critical component of rational drug therapy. Community pharmacists are in a unique position to track whether patients are refilling their prescriptions on time and to identify any barriers to adherence, such as side effects, forgetfulness, or confusion about the dosing regimen. Pharmacists can provide strategies to improve adherence, such as setting up medication reminders, offering pill organizers, or simplifying dosing schedules when possible.

Regular follow-up with patients allows pharmacists to assess the effectiveness of the therapy and make necessary adjustments in collaboration with the prescribing physician. For instance, if a patient reports persistent side effects or insufficient symptom relief, the pharmacist can suggest a dosage adjustment or a different medication to the physician. This ongoing support helps ensure that patients achieve the best possible outcomes from their treatment.

Public Health Advocacy and Community Education

Community pharmacists also contribute to public health by advocating for the rational use of medicines and educating the community about important health issues. This includes providing information on the proper use of over-the-counter (OTC) medications, the risks of self-medication, and the importance of vaccinations and preventive care.

For example, during flu season, a pharmacist might educate patients on the benefits of getting a flu vaccine and the importance of using OTC medications appropriately to manage symptoms without overuse or misuse. By raising awareness and promoting safe medication practices, pharmacists help prevent medication-related problems and improve overall public health.

Collaboration with Healthcare Providers

Effective rational drug therapy often requires collaboration between pharmacists and other healthcare providers, such as physicians, nurses, and specialists. Pharmacists contribute their expertise in pharmacotherapy to ensure that drug regimens are tailored to the individual needs of patients. This interdisciplinary approach is particularly important in managing complex cases, such as patients with multiple chronic conditions or those requiring polypharmacy.

For instance, a pharmacist working with a healthcare team in a community health center might participate in case reviews or medication therapy management (MTM) sessions to discuss the best therapeutic options for patients with complex medication regimens. This collaborative effort helps optimize patient care and ensures that all aspects of the patient's health are considered in treatment decisions.

12.2.2 Promoting Rational Drug Use

Promoting rational drug use is a fundamental component of healthcare, aimed at ensuring that medications are prescribed, dispensed, and consumed in a manner that maximizes therapeutic effectiveness, minimizes risks, and is cost-efficient. Rational drug use involves prescribing the right drug, in the correct dose, for the appropriate duration, and at an affordable price, with active participation from both healthcare providers and patients.

The promotion of rational drug use is essential to combating the misuse of medications, which can lead to adverse drug reactions, increased healthcare costs, and the development of drug-resistant pathogens.

Educating Healthcare Providers

One of the key strategies for promoting rational drug use is the continuous education of healthcare providers, including physicians, pharmacists, and nurses. Healthcare providers must be well-informed about the principles of rational drug therapy, the latest clinical guidelines, and the evidence-based use of medications. Regular training and updates on new drugs, therapeutic protocols, and the management of common conditions are essential to ensure that providers prescribe drugs appropriately and responsibly.

For example, workshops, seminars, and online courses on rational prescribing practices can help healthcare providers stay updated on the most effective treatments for various diseases. Such educational initiatives can also address the challenges of polypharmacy, particularly in elderly patients or those with multiple chronic conditions, where the risk of drug interactions and adverse effects is high.

Developing and Implementing Treatment Guidelines

The development and implementation of standardized treatment guidelines are critical in promoting rational drug use. These guidelines, often based on the World Health Organization (WHO) recommendations and national health policies, provide a framework for the appropriate use of medications in the treatment of specific conditions. They help ensure that healthcare providers follow best practices in prescribing, thereby reducing the variability in treatment and improving patient outcomes.

For instance, national or regional health authorities may develop guidelines for the treatment of common conditions such as hypertension, diabetes, or infections. These guidelines typically include first-line and second-line treatment options, dosing recommendations, and monitoring requirements, helping to ensure that patients receive the most effective and safe therapy.

Rational Prescribing Practices

Rational prescribing is at the heart of rational drug use. It involves the careful selection of medications based on the patient's clinical needs, preferences, and circumstances. Healthcare providers should prescribe medications only when necessary, avoiding the overuse or inappropriate use of drugs that can lead to adverse effects or unnecessary costs.

For example, the use of antibiotics should be restricted to cases where there is clear evidence of a bacterial infection, and not for viral infections such as the common cold, where antibiotics are ineffective. By following rational prescribing practices, healthcare providers can help reduce the emergence of antibiotic resistance, which is a major global health threat.

Patient Education and Empowerment

Educating patients about their medications and involving them in decision-making is crucial for promoting rational drug use. Patients who understand the purpose of their medications, how to take them correctly, and the importance of adherence are more likely to use their medications rationally. This, in turn, improves therapeutic outcomes and reduces the risk of medication errors.

Pharmacists play a vital role in patient education, providing clear instructions on how to use medications, discussing potential side effects, and advising on how to manage missed doses. For instance, a pharmacist might explain to a patient with diabetes the importance of taking insulin as prescribed, monitoring blood glucose levels regularly, and recognizing signs of hypoglycemia.

Monitoring and Evaluation

The monitoring and evaluation of drug use within healthcare systems are essential to identify patterns of irrational drug use and to implement corrective measures. This can involve regular audits of prescription practices, tracking the use of high-risk medications, and analyzing drug utilization data to detect any inappropriate use or overuse of medications.

For example, a hospital pharmacy might conduct an audit of antibiotic prescriptions to ensure that they are being used appropriately, in line with treatment guidelines. If the audit reveals that antibiotics are being overprescribed, the hospital can implement targeted interventions, such as additional training for prescribers or the introduction of an antibiotic stewardship program.

Public Health Campaigns

Public health campaigns aimed at promoting rational drug use can raise awareness among the general population about the risks of self-medication, the importance of following prescription instructions, and the dangers of using counterfeit or substandard drugs. These campaigns can also address specific issues, such as the overuse of antibiotics, by educating the public about the consequences of antibiotic resistance.

For instance, a national campaign might focus on educating parents about the appropriate use of medications for their children, emphasizing the importance of consulting healthcare providers before giving any medications and discouraging the use of leftover or shared medications.

Collaboration with Regulatory Authorities

Regulatory authorities play a crucial role in promoting rational drug use by ensuring that only safe, effective, and high-quality medications are available on the market. They are responsible for the approval and monitoring of drugs, the enforcement of prescription regulations, and the prevention of counterfeit medicines.

Healthcare providers and pharmacists can collaborate with regulatory authorities by reporting adverse drug reactions, participating in pharmacovigilance programs, and supporting efforts to regulate the marketing and distribution of medications. For example, pharmacists can report cases of counterfeit drugs to the authorities, helping to protect the public from potentially harmful products.

THIRTEEN

CODE OF ETHICS FOR COMMUNITY PHARMACISTS

13.1 Ethical Principles in Community Pharmacy

Ethical principles are the foundation of professional practice in community pharmacy, guiding pharmacists in their interactions with patients, healthcare providers, and society. These principles ensure that pharmacists maintain the highest standards of care, prioritize the well-being of their patients, and uphold the integrity of the profession. The code of ethics for community pharmacists outlines these principles, providing a framework for ethical decision-making in various aspects of pharmacy practice.

Beneficence and Non-Maleficence

The principles of beneficence and non-maleficence are central to the ethical practice of pharmacy. Beneficence refers to the obligation to act in the best interest of the patient, ensuring that all actions taken by the pharmacist are intended to promote the patient's health and well-being. This involves providing accurate information, ensuring the safe and effective use of medications, and offering guidance on health-related issues. For example, a pharmacist might take the time to counsel a patient on the correct use of an inhaler, ensuring that the patient understands how to use it properly to manage their asthma effectively.

Non-maleficence, on the other hand, is the duty to do no harm. Pharmacists must take all necessary precautions to prevent harm to their patients, whether through the dispensing of medications, providing advice, or any other professional activity. This includes avoiding errors in dispensing, ensuring that medications are appropriate for the patient's condition, and being vigilant about potential drug interactions. For instance, a pharmacist must check for possible contraindications before dispensing a new medication to a patient who is already on multiple drugs.

Autonomy

Respect for patient autonomy is another key ethical principle in community pharmacy. Autonomy involves recognizing and respecting the right of patients to make informed decisions about their healthcare. Pharmacists must provide patients with all the necessary information regarding their medications, including potential benefits, risks, and alternatives, allowing patients to make informed choices about their treatment. For example, when discussing a new prescription with a patient, the pharmacist should explain the purpose of the medication, how it works, and any possible side effects, enabling the patient to decide whether to proceed with the treatment.

Pharmacists must also respect patients' decisions, even if they differ from the pharmacist's recommendations, as long as those decisions do not result in harm. This respect for autonomy extends to ensuring confidentiality and privacy in all interactions with patients, which is essential for maintaining trust and fostering open communication.

Justice

The principle of justice in community pharmacy pertains to fairness in the distribution of healthcare resources and the provision of care. Pharmacists have a duty to treat all patients fairly and equitably, regardless of their background, socioeconomic status, or personal beliefs. This includes providing equal access to medications, information, and services, as well as advocating for the needs of vulnerable populations who may face barriers to accessing care.

For instance, a pharmacist might work to ensure that essential medications are available at an affordable price or collaborate with community organizations to provide services to underserved populations. Justice also involves addressing any disparities in healthcare and working to eliminate them, such as by ensuring that all patients receive the same quality of care and attention, regardless of their ability to pay.

Confidentiality

Confidentiality is a cornerstone of the pharmacist-patient relationship, requiring pharmacists to protect the privacy of patient information at all times. Pharmacists must ensure that all patient records, medication histories, and other personal health information are kept secure and only shared with authorized individuals. Breaches of confidentiality can undermine patient trust and compromise the quality of care.

For example, when discussing a patient's medication regimen in a community pharmacy, the pharmacist should ensure that the conversation takes place in a private area where others cannot overhear. Additionally, pharmacists must be careful when handling electronic health records, ensuring that access is restricted to those who need it for the provision of care.

Fidelity

Fidelity involves maintaining loyalty and commitment to the patient, fulfilling all professional obligations, and adhering to the ethical standards of the profession. Pharmacists must act with integrity, honesty, and transparency in all their professional interactions. This includes honoring commitments made to patients, such as following up on medication-related concerns, and providing accurate and truthful information.

For instance, if a pharmacist promises to check with a physician about a potential drug interaction and follow up with the patient, they must ensure that this promise is kept. Fidelity also extends to the professional duty of pharmacists to continuously update their knowledge and skills, ensuring that they provide the best possible care based on the latest evidence and guidelines.

Accountability

Accountability is the ethical obligation of pharmacists to take responsibility for their actions and decisions. Pharmacists must be willing to explain and justify their professional conduct, particularly in situations where ethical dilemmas arise. This involves being transparent about the rationale behind treatment recommendations, acknowledging any mistakes, and taking steps to correct them.

For example, if a pharmacist realizes that an incorrect medication was dispensed, they must promptly inform the patient, rectify the error, and take measures to prevent similar incidents in the future. Accountability also involves participating in continuing professional development and engaging in reflective practice to improve the quality of care provided.

13.2 Professional Conduct and Responsibilities

Professional conduct and responsibilities are critical components of the ethical framework within which community pharmacists operate. These elements define the standards of behavior expected of pharmacists and ensure that they fulfill their roles with integrity, competence, and respect for the trust placed in them by patients, colleagues, and the wider community. Upholding these standards is essential for maintaining the credibility of the profession and ensuring that pharmacists contribute positively to public health.

Adherence to Legal and Ethical Standards

Community pharmacists must adhere to both legal and ethical standards in their practice. This involves complying with all relevant laws and regulations governing the dispensing of medications, maintaining accurate records, and ensuring the safe storage and handling of pharmaceuticals. Pharmacists are also expected to stay informed about changes in laws and regulations that impact their practice and to adjust their procedures accordingly.

For example, a pharmacist must ensure that controlled substances are dispensed according to legal requirements, with proper documentation and safeguards in place to prevent misuse. Additionally, pharmacists must follow ethical guidelines, such as avoiding conflicts of interest, not engaging in fraudulent activities, and ensuring that their actions are always in the best interest of the patient.

Competence and Continuous Professional Development

Competence is a fundamental responsibility for all healthcare professionals, including pharmacists. It requires that pharmacists possess the necessary knowledge, skills, and judgment to perform their duties effectively. This includes staying current with advancements in pharmaceutical science, changes in clinical guidelines, and the introduction of new medications or therapies.

To maintain and enhance their competence, pharmacists must engage in continuous professional development (CPD). This involves participating in ongoing education, attending workshops, conferences, and training sessions, and actively seeking opportunities to improve their practice. For instance, a pharmacist might attend a seminar on the latest developments in diabetes management to ensure they can provide the best possible care to patients with this condition.

Patient-Centered Care

Providing patient-centered care is a core responsibility of community pharmacists. This approach involves placing the needs, preferences, and values of the patient at the forefront of all healthcare decisions. Pharmacists must take the time to listen to their patients, understand their concerns, and provide personalized advice and treatment options that align with the patient's individual circumstances.

For example, when counseling a patient on a new medication, a pharmacist should consider the patient's lifestyle, potential barriers to adherence, and any concerns the patient may have about side effects. By doing so, the pharmacist can help ensure that the treatment plan is both effective and acceptable to the patient, thereby improving health outcomes.

Communication and Collaboration

Effective communication is essential in pharmacy practice, both in interactions with patients and in collaboration with other healthcare professionals. Pharmacists must be able to convey information clearly and accurately, ensuring that patients understand how to use their medications safely and effectively. This includes explaining complex medical information in a way that is accessible and comprehensible to individuals with varying levels of health literacy.

In addition to patient communication, pharmacists must collaborate with other members of the healthcare team, such as physicians, nurses, and specialists, to ensure coordinated care. For instance, a pharmacist might work with a physician to adjust a patient's medication regimen based on the patient's response to treatment or to address potential drug interactions. Such collaboration is key to providing holistic and integrated care.

Confidentiality and Privacy

Respecting patient confidentiality and privacy is a fundamental aspect of professional conduct in pharmacy practice. Pharmacists are entrusted with sensitive health information and must take all necessary measures to protect this information from unauthorized access or disclosure. This includes adhering to legal requirements related to data protection and ensuring that all patient interactions and records are handled with discretion.

For example, when discussing a patient's medication or health condition, the pharmacist should do so in a private setting where the conversation cannot be overheard by others. Additionally, electronic health records should be securely stored, with access limited to authorized personnel only.

Ethical Decision-Making

Pharmacists frequently encounter situations that require ethical decision-making. These situations may involve conflicts of interest, dilemmas regarding the appropriate course of action, or challenges in balancing the needs of the patient with broader public health considerations. Pharmacists must use their professional judgment, guided by ethical principles, to navigate these situations and make decisions that are in the best interest of the patient while upholding the integrity of the profession.

For instance, a pharmacist might face a situation where a patient requests an early refill of a controlled medication, raising concerns about potential misuse. In such cases, the pharmacist must carefully consider the ethical implications, consult relevant guidelines, and take appropriate action, which may include discussing the situation with the patient, contacting the prescribing physician, or refusing the refill if necessary.

Accountability and Transparency

Accountability is a key responsibility for pharmacists, requiring them to take responsibility for their actions and decisions. This involves being transparent with patients about the risks and benefits of treatments, acknowledging and correcting any errors, and being open to feedback. Pharmacists must also document their decisions and actions accurately, ensuring that there is a clear record of the care provided.

For example, if a pharmacist realizes that an error was made in dispensing a medication, they must promptly inform the patient, correct the error, and take steps to prevent similar incidents in the future. By being accountable, pharmacists demonstrate their commitment to patient safety and the ethical practice of their profession.

13.3 Dealing with Ethical Dilemmas

Ethical dilemmas are complex situations in which community pharmacists must make difficult decisions, often involving a conflict between ethical principles, professional responsibilities, and patient care. These dilemmas can arise in various aspects of pharmacy practice, from dispensing medications to managing patient confidentiality, and require pharmacists to carefully consider the potential consequences of their actions. Dealing with ethical dilemmas effectively requires a deep understanding of ethical principles, critical thinking, and the ability to navigate challenging situations with integrity and compassion.

Identifying Ethical Dilemmas

The first step in dealing with ethical dilemmas is recognizing when such a situation exists. Ethical dilemmas often involve conflicting duties or values, such as the need to respect patient autonomy while also ensuring patient safety. For example, a pharmacist may encounter a situation where a patient insists on a treatment that the pharmacist believes is not in the patient's best interest. In such cases, the pharmacist must identify the ethical conflict, which may involve balancing the principle of autonomy with the principle of non-maleficence (doing no harm).

Ethical dilemmas can also arise from issues related to resource allocation, where a pharmacist must decide how to distribute limited medications fairly among patients, or from potential conflicts of interest, where a pharmacist's personal or financial interests may conflict with their professional duties.

Ethical Decision-Making Framework

Once an ethical dilemma has been identified, pharmacists can use an ethical decision-making framework to guide their actions. This framework typically involves several key steps:

1. **Gathering Information**: The pharmacist should gather all relevant information about the situation, including the patient's medical history, the potential benefits and risks of the available options, and any relevant legal or professional guidelines. This comprehensive understanding of the situation is essential for making an informed decision.
2. **Identifying the Ethical Issues**: The pharmacist must clearly identify the ethical issues involved in the dilemma. This includes determining which ethical principles are in conflict, such as patient autonomy, beneficence, non-maleficence, justice, and confidentiality.
3. **Considering the Options**: The pharmacist should consider all possible courses of action, evaluating each option in terms of its ethical implications and potential outcomes. This step involves weighing the benefits and risks of each option, as well as considering the long-term consequences for the patient, the pharmacist, and the broader community.
4. **Consulting with Others**: Ethical dilemmas are often complex, and it can be helpful to consult with colleagues, supervisors, or ethical committees to gain different perspectives and insights. This collaborative approach can provide valuable support and help ensure that the decision is well-reasoned and justifiable.

5. **Making the Decision**: After carefully considering all the information and options, the pharmacist must make a decision that aligns with ethical principles and professional standards. The decision should prioritize the patient's well-being while also considering the broader implications for society and the profession.
6. **Implementing the Decision**: Once a decision has been made, the pharmacist must implement it in a manner that is respectful and considerate of the patient's needs and feelings. This may involve explaining the decision to the patient, providing additional support, or making necessary referrals.
7. **Reflecting on the Outcome**: After the decision has been implemented, it is important for the pharmacist to reflect on the outcome and consider whether the decision achieved the desired results. Reflection allows the pharmacist to learn from the experience and improve their approach to future ethical dilemmas.

Examples of Ethical Dilemmas in Community Pharmacy

Ethical dilemmas in community pharmacy can take many forms. Some common examples include:

- **Patient Confidentiality vs. Public Safety**: A pharmacist may encounter a situation where maintaining patient confidentiality could potentially endanger public safety. For example, if a patient with a contagious disease refuses to inform others who may be at risk, the pharmacist must decide whether to breach confidentiality to protect the public.
- **Resource Allocation**: During shortages of essential medications, a pharmacist may need to decide how to allocate limited supplies. This could involve making difficult choices about which patients receive the medication based on factors such as medical need, likelihood of benefit, or the urgency of the condition.
- **Conflicts of Interest**: A pharmacist who owns or is financially invested in a pharmacy may face a conflict of interest when deciding whether to stock or recommend certain medications. The ethical dilemma arises if the pharmacist feels pressured to prioritize profit over patient care.
- **End-of-Life Care**: A pharmacist may be asked to dispense medications for end-of-life care that could hasten a patient's death, such as in palliative sedation or physician-assisted dying (where legal). The pharmacist must navigate the ethical challenges of respecting the patient's wishes while

considering their own moral beliefs and professional responsibilities.

Ethical Leadership and Advocacy

Pharmacists are not only responsible for resolving individual ethical dilemmas but also for promoting an ethical culture within their practice and the wider healthcare system. This involves advocating for policies and practices that support ethical decision-making, such as promoting access to essential medicines, ensuring equitable care, and upholding patient rights.

Ethical leadership also requires pharmacists to serve as role models for ethical behavior, demonstrating a commitment to ethical principles in their daily practice. By fostering an environment where ethical considerations are valued and openly discussed, pharmacists can contribute to a more ethical and compassionate healthcare system.

In conclusion, dealing with ethical dilemmas in community pharmacy requires a structured approach that prioritizes ethical principles, patient well-being, and professional integrity. Through careful consideration, consultation, and reflection, pharmacists can navigate these complex situations and make decisions that uphold the highest standards of ethical practice. By promoting an ethical culture and advocating for just and equitable care, pharmacists play a crucial role in maintaining the trust and confidence of the patients and communities they serve.

FOURTEEN
BIBLIOGRAPHY

Books:

1. **Remington: The Science and Practice of Pharmacy.** 21st Edition. Edited by Loyd V. Allen, Jr., et al. Philadelphia: Lippincott Williams & Wilkins, 2006.
2. **Goodman & Gilman's: The Pharmacological Basis of Therapeutics.** 12th Edition. Edited by Laurence Brunton, et al. New York: McGraw-Hill, 2011.
3. **Pharmaceutical Practice.** 5th Edition. Edited by A.J. Winfield, R.M.E. Richards, and P.J. Meeson. Edinburgh: Churchill Livingstone, 2013.
4. **Community Pharmacy: Symptoms, Diagnosis and Treatment.** 3rd Edition. Edited by Paul Rutter. Edinburgh: Elsevier Health Sciences, 2013.
5. **Clinical Pharmacy and Therapeutics.** 5th Edition. Edited by Roger Walker and Cate Whittlesea. Edinburgh: Churchill Livingstone, 2012.
6. **Aulton's Pharmaceutics: The Design and Manufacture of Medicines.** 5th Edition. Edited by Michael E. Aulton and Kevin M.G. Taylor. Edinburgh: Elsevier, 2018.
7. **Pharmacy Management: Essentials for All Practice Settings.** 4th Edition. Edited by Shane P. Desselle and David P. Zgarrick. New York: McGraw-Hill Education, 2016.
8. **Applied Therapeutics: The Clinical Use of Drugs.** 11th Edition. Edited by Brian Katcher and Richard R. Wilkinson. Philadelphia: Wolters Kluwer, 2020.
9. **Patient Assessment in Pharmacy Practice.** 3rd Edition. By Rhonda M. Jones, Raymond L. Weitzel, and Kathryn R. Ely. Philadelphia: Lippincott Williams & Wilkins, 2012.

10. **Pharmaceutical Calculations.** 14th Edition. By Howard C. Ansel and Shelly J. Stockton. Baltimore: Lippincott Williams & Wilkins, 2016.

Journals:

1. **American Journal of Health-System Pharmacy**
2. **Journal of the American Pharmacists Association**
3. **Pharmacotherapy: The Journal of Human Pharmacology and Drug Therapy**
4. **International Journal of Clinical Pharmacy**
5. **Journal of Pharmaceutical Health Services Research**
6. **Annals of Pharmacotherapy**
7. **British Journal of Clinical Pharmacology**
8. **European Journal of Clinical Pharmacy**
9. **Journal of Pharmacy Practice and Research**
10. **Indian Journal of Pharmaceutical Sciences**

Websites:

1. **World Health Organization (WHO).**www.who.int
2. **Pharmacy Council of India.** www.pci.nic.in
3. **National Institute for Health and Care Excellence (NICE).**www.nice.org.uk
4. **Centers for Disease Control and Prevention (CDC).**www.cdc.gov
5. **Food and Drug Administration (FDA).**www.fda.gov
6. **National Health Service (NHS).**www.nhs.uk
7. **U.S. Pharmacopeia (USP).**www.usp.org
8. **Drugs.com.**www.drugs.com
9. **Medscape.**www.medscape.com
10. **Mayo Clinic.**www.mayoclinic.org

Guidelines and Government Documents:

1. **Ministry of Health and Family Welfare, Government of India.** "The Drugs and Cosmetics Act, 1940 and The Drugs and Cosmetics Rules, 1945."
2. **Pharmacy Practice Regulations, 2015.** Pharmacy Council of India.
3. **WHO.** "Pharmacovigilance: Ensuring the Safe Use of Medicines."
4. **National List of Essential Medicines (NLEM), India.**

5. **FDA.** "Guidance for Industry: Good Clinical Practice (GCP)."
6. **National Health Policy 2017.** Ministry of Health and Family Welfare, India.
7. **Good Pharmacy Practice Guidelines.** World Health Organization.
8. **Indian Pharmacopoeia.** Indian Pharmacopoeia Commission.
9. **The Narcotic Drugs and Psychotropic Substances Act, 1985.**
10. **Clinical Establishments (Registration and Regulation) Act, 2010.**

Conference Papers:

1. **"Advances in Community Pharmacy Practice."** Paper presented at the International Conference on Pharmaceutical Sciences, New Delhi, India, 2023.
2. **Shah, R. V.** "Role of Community Pharmacists in Patient Care." Presented at the Annual Conference of Indian Pharmacists Association, Mumbai, India, 2024.
3. **"Pharmacovigilance and the Role of Community Pharmacists."** Paper presented at the International Congress on Pharmacology, Bengaluru, India, 2022.
4. **Patel, S. M.** "Innovations in Drug Dispensing and Patient Safety." Presented at the Global Summit on Clinical Pharmacy, Hyderabad, India, 2023.
5. **"Ethics in Pharmacy Practice."** Presented at the National Seminar on Healthcare Ethics, Chennai, India, 2024.

Reports:

1. **National Pharmaceutical Regulatory Authority.** "Annual Report on Pharmacy Practice and Standards." Kuala Lumpur: NPRA, 2023.
2. **World Health Organization.** "Global Report on Essential Medicines." WHO, 2024.
3. **Pharmacy Council of India.** "Annual Report 2024: Trends in Pharmacy Education and Practice."
4. **Ministry of Health and Family Welfare.** "National Health Profile 2024."
5. **Indian Pharmacopoeia Commission.** "Annual Report 2024."

FIFTEEN

ABOUT AUTHORS

Dr Challa srinivas Reddy, principal & Professor at Vaagdevi college of pharmacy Ramnagar Hanamkonda warangal telangana. Boasts over 19 years of extensive experience in pharmaceutical education and leadership. He holds a Ph.D. in Pharmaceutical sciences from Kakatiya Universty ,warangal,telangana. Dr. Challa srinivas Reddy has published numerous articles in reputed journals and presented at numerous national and international platforms, focusing on advancements in community pharmacy and Herbal Drug technology.

Recognized with several awards for excellence in teachingand research he is the reciepnt of ugc -SRF from UGC New Delhi,he is a member of APTI,IPA and a mentor to graduate students, shaping future professionals in the pharmaceutical sciences.

Dr.B.S.Sharvana Bhava, Professor & Head, Department of Clinical Pharmacy &Pharm.D., Vaagdevi College of Pharmacy, Ramnagar, Hanumakonda, Telangana, India, is a forerunner in the field of Clinical Pharmacy and Pharmacology, with a Ph.D in Pharmaceutical Sciences and M.Sc in Psychology. Dr.Sharvana bhava with over 13 years of teaching & research experience, handling various subjects such as Human Anatomy & Physiology, Pathophysiology, Pharmacology, PharmacotherapeuticsI,II,&III, Clinical Pharmacy, Community Pharmacy, Hospital Pharmacy, Research Methodology, Clinical Toxicology, Clinical Research and also completed over 42 projects of Pharm.D. students in Clinical aspects of the research.

Dr.Sharvana bhava has authored over 50 publications of his research in various National & International peer reviewed journals. He has also authored a text book named "Textbook on Clinical Research", which is very useful for the students aspiring towards the research.

Dr. Sharvana bhava has received "Best Preceptor award", Best Oral Presentations, Best Poster Presentations and many awards for his excellent contributions in various areas.

He is a member of APTI, Guide & Mentor for the Pharm.D. students and helping in shaping the students towards the excellence in their endeavours.

Dr. Santhi Sree Vemulapalli, Professor at Vijaya College of Pharmacy, Hayathnagar, Munagnoor, India, boasts over 16 years of extensive experience in pharmaceutical education and leadership. She holds a Ph.D. in Pharmaceutics from Acharya Nagarjuna University, Guntur. Dr. Santhi Sree has published numerous articles in reputed journals and presented at numerous national and international platforms, focusing on advancements in drug delivery systems and nanotechnology. Recognized with several awards for excellence in teaching, she is a member of APTI and a mentor to graduate students, shaping future professionals in the pharmaceutical sciences.

www.ingramcontent.com/pod-product-compliance
Ingram Content Group UK Ltd.
Pitfield, Milton Keynes, MK11 3LW, UK
UKHW062311290726
14090UKWH00018B/1002

9 798895 443606